The Beginner's

Blueprint to Forex Trading

By

Nathan Venture, D

WELL-BEING
PUBLISHING

The Beginner's
Blueprint to Forex Trading

Table of Contents

Introduction

Welcome to the world of Forex trading—a dynamic and exhilarating field that promises opportunities for those willing to learn. This introduction isn't just about familiarizing you with the basic concepts; it aims to give you the confidence to step into the Forex market with clarity and purpose. No previous experience is necessary to embark on this journey. All it takes is an open mind and a willingness to learn.

Forex, a term derived from "foreign exchange," is the largest financial market in the world. It's a place where currencies are traded, and its vastness can be daunting for newcomers. However, with the right understanding and tools, it can also be a rewarding arena for those who approach it thoughtfully. The primary objective of this book is to demystify the complexities of Forex trading and equip you with foundational knowledge, so you can make informed decisions.

The Forex market is unique in several ways. Unlike stock markets, which operate within fixed hours, the Forex market is open 24 hours a day, five days a week. This allows traders flexibility in choosing when they want to interact with the market, according to their schedule and strategies. We'll explore more on this exciting feature and others as we progress through the chapters.

Before diving into the intricate details, let's set our expectations straight. Trading Forex isn't about making a quick fortune; it's about developing a skill set that can lead to consistent success over time. Patience, discipline, and continuous learning are crucial attributes that differentiate successful traders from the rest. As you delve into this book, you'll find strategies not only for starting out but also for evolving as a trader.

You'll soon discover that understanding Forex trading fundamentals is a lot like learning a new language. You need to get familiar with the basic vocabulary—currency pairs, pips, leverage, and margin. Like building blocks, these terms and concepts form the foundation upon which profitable trading strategies are built. Each chapter of this book is designed to guide you meticulously through these foundational elements, ensuring you gain a comprehensive understanding without feeling overwhelmed.

One of the most fascinating aspects of the Forex market is its ever-changing nature. Pair that with a global reach, and you have a market that's influenced by a myriad of factors, from economic reports and geopolitical events to market sentiment and technical analysis. Understanding these variables and how they interact is essential for making informed trading decisions. As you advance through this book, you'll learn to analyze market conditions and adapt to its shifts, turning challenges into opportunities.

This book isn't just about facts and figures; it's designed to inspire and motivate. You'll find stories of traders who began just like you and have found success through persistence and strategy. The lessons from their journey can serve as a guide and a motivator, proving that informed trading, coupled with determination, can yield wonderful results.

By the end of this introduction and the book as a whole, you'll be armed with the tools and knowledge you need to embark on your trading journey. More than that, you'll have the confidence to navigate the Forex market, not as a novice, but as a well-informed participant ready to make strategic decisions.

So, take a deep breath and commit to this learning adventure. The Forex market is vast and ever-evolving, but with dedication to understanding and applying the concepts in this book, you're already on the path to becoming a competent Forex trader. Remember, knowledge is your greatest asset in the world of Forex trading, and this book is here to provide that for you.

Chapter 1: Understanding Forex Trading

In the vast world of financial markets, understanding Forex trading is your first step towards uncovering a dynamic and potentially rewarding arena. Forex, or foreign exchange, involves the buying and selling of currency pairs where currencies are exchanged in the hope of profiting from fluctuations in exchange rates. It's a global market, operating 24 hours a day and offering ample flexibility to traders worldwide. Currency pairs are typically quoted in 'pips', a term you will soon find to be part of your everyday trading vocabulary, representing the smallest change in value between two currencies. You'll learn the significance of leverage, a tool that amplifies potential gains but also requires careful risk management to avoid losses. Grasping margin, which ensures you have sufficient capital in your account to cover potential losses, is also vital. With this foundational knowledge, you're ready to delve deeper into the mechanics of Forex trading, setting the stage for making informed and confident trading decisions.

What Is Forex Trading?

Forex trading, short for foreign exchange trading, involves buying and selling currencies on a global market. If you've ever traveled to another country and exchanged your currency for local money, you've participated, albeit unofficially, in the world of forex. At its core, forex trading provides businesses, governments, and individuals with the means to convert one currency into another, facilitating international trade and investment.

The forex market stands out because it's the largest and most liquid financial market in the world. It's not confined to a central marketplace but is instead conducted over the counter (OTC) through a global network of computers. This setup allows the market to operate 24 hours a day, five days a week across major financial centers in nearly every time zone. This continuous nature means that the market is always active somewhere in the world, with prices constantly changing in response to a multitude of factors.

Understanding the basics of forex trading begins with grasping the concept of currency pairs. In the forex market, currencies are traded in pairs. The first currency in the pair is the base currency, and the second is the quote currency. For instance, in the currency pair EUR/USD, the euro (EUR) is the base currency, and the US dollar (USD) is the quote currency. The price of the pair represents how much of the quote currency is needed to purchase one unit of the base currency.

Forex trading is about anticipating how these currency pairs will move. Traders might buy (or go long on) a currency pair if they think the base currency will strengthen against the quote currency. Conversely, they might sell (or go short) if they predict the base currency will weaken. This decision-making process often involves a combination of technical analysis and fundamental analysis, informed by economic indicators, geopolitical events, and market sentiment.

A significant aspect that distinguishes forex trading from other financial markets is the concept of leverage. Leverage in the forex market allows traders to control a larger position with a smaller amount of actual capital. This concept can significantly amplify profits, but it's a double-edged sword—losses can be magnified too. Understanding leverage and using it wisely is a critical aspect of becoming a successful forex trader.

For those new to the forex market, the idea of trading global currencies might seem daunting. However, it's an endeavor that's accessible, thanks in part to online trading platforms, demo accounts, and a wealth of educational resources. Many brokers offer platforms that allow beginners to practice trading with virtual money, building confidence and understanding without financial risk.

The allure of forex trading often lies in its flexibility, requiring only a computer and an internet connection to get started. Unlike more traditional forms of investing, forex doesn't necessitate a large amount of initial capital, making it particularly attractive to retail traders looking to diversify their investment strategies.

Despite its accessibility, forex trading is not without risk. Price fluctuations can occur swiftly, influenced by world events, economic releases, and trader sentiment. As such, it's crucial for anyone entering the forex market to employ sound risk management techniques. This involves setting stop-loss orders, managing trading capital wisely, and maintaining emotional discipline.

To succeed in forex trading, one must not only understand the mechanics of the market but also develop a strategic approach. A well-thought-out trading plan is essential, outlining personal goals, trading style, and risk appetite. It's a dynamic and evolving market, and staying informed about global news, economic developments, and market trends is paramount.

Ultimately, the journey into forex trading is a continuous learning process. As the market evolves, so too should your strategies and knowledge. Many traders find value in networking with other traders, learning from shared experiences, and remaining open to new insights and methods.

Forex trading can be both rewarding and challenging. It's a field that combines analytical thinking with the ability to adapt quickly to changing market conditions. With determination, an open mind, and a solid grasp of the basics, you can navigate the forex market with increased confidence and make informed decisions that align with your financial goals.

History of the Forex Market

The history of the Forex market is a fascinating journey that spans centuries, evolving through a series of remarkable events and institutional shifts. Understanding this historical progression helps us appreciate how the Forex market became the largest and most liquid financial market today. It's a tale that starts with ancient barter systems, takes intriguing turns through the emergence of coins and paper money, and continues into the technologically advanced global network we know today.

The concept of currency exchange dates back to ancient times. Bartering was the earliest form of trade among different cultures, a method constrained by its direct exchange limitations—goods for goods—requiring a mutually beneficial agreement. The introduction of coins in the 6th century BC by the Lydians marked a significant leap forward. Coins offered a standardized medium of exchange, paving the way for more complex trading systems.

As societies grew and economies became more interconnected, the need for currency trading became apparent. The Roman Empire played a crucial role in refining currency systems, establishing a monetary economy that facilitated international trade across its vast territories. Following the fall of Rome, Europe experienced several currency transitions, but the essence of trade persisted, evolving with each era.

Fast forward to the Middle Ages, the Medici family in Italy established the first foreign exchange market. They opened banks in foreign locations to trade currencies and funded international trade through bills of exchange. This ingenious system allowed merchants to deliver goods without directly exchanging physical currency, mitigating some risks of transporting gold or silver across borders.

The next significant milestone arrived in the early 19th century with the adoption of the Gold Standard. Countries pegged their currencies to a specific amount of gold, enabling a fixed exchange rate system. This period marked the beginning of a more controlled and predictable global trading system. However, the Gold Standard had its constraints and fell during the economic pressures of World War I, leading to a more flexible monetary system.

The aftermath of World War II brought further change. The Bretton Woods Conference in 1944 was a landmark moment, giving rise to the Bretton Woods system. This agreement established the US dollar as the world's reserve currency, backed by gold, limiting currency fluctuations and fostering international trade stability. The International Monetary Fund and the World Bank, both pivotal institutions in global finance, were created during this conference.

The Bretton Woods system served well until the early 1970s. The growing US involvement in the Vietnam War and resultant fiscal policies strained the US gold reserves, culminating in President Nixon's decision to suspend the dollar's convertibility into gold in 1971. This shift effectively ended the Bretton Woods system, leading to the modern era of floating exchange rates, which characterizes the contemporary Forex market.

The emergence of computer technology in the late 20th century revolutionized Forex trading. The development of electronic trading platforms democratized access, enabling a broader range of participants to enter the market. Traders no longer needed to be physically present in trading hubs, as transactions could occur instantaneously from anywhere with an internet connection. This leap in technology increased market liquidity, competition, and ultimately, market efficiency.

Today, the Forex market is a global network operating through banks, financial institutions, corporations, and individual traders across time zones. The market operates 24 hours a day, closing over $6 trillion in average daily turnover. This astounding volume reflects the importance of currencies in global trade, investment, and financial speculation.

Various factors continue to influence the Forex market, from geopolitical events and economic policies to large-scale economic shifts like Brexit or the emergence of cryptocurrencies. Each event adds a new chapter to this ever-evolving market, providing both challenges and opportunities for traders worldwide. The adaptation to these dynamics speaks volumes about the resilience and flexibility that have been hallmarks of the Forex market throughout history.

In learning about the history of the Forex market, you're not merely engaging with a chronological account; you're understanding the foundations that modern trading practices are built upon. This insight is indispensable for anyone looking to embark on the Forex trading journey. The story of Forex trading shows us how intertwined global economies are and how this interconnectedness drives everyone—traders, businesses, and governments—through cycles of opportunity and growth.

Key Advantages of Trading Forex

Engaging in Forex trading opens the door to a realm filled with possibilities and opportunities unlike any other financial market. At its core, Forex trading stands out for its unparalleled accessibility and the unique potential it offers to both novice and seasoned traders. The global reach of the Forex market ensures it operates 24 hours a day, five days a week, allowing traders from all corners of the world to participate at times that best suit their schedules.

The first of these advantages lies in the market's immense liquidity. Forex is the most liquid financial market in the world, with trillions of dollars being traded daily. This high level of liquidity is key to ensuring price stability and narrow bid-ask spreads, which means traders can enter and exit positions with ease, often without significant changes in price. For newcomers, this means that the currency pairs you're interested in can almost always be traded without having to wait.

Moreover, Forex trading is embraced for its minimal entry barriers. You don't need a big bank roll to start trading; with the advent of micro and mini accounts, even those who are just dipping their toes into trading can begin with as little as $50. This accessibility means that Forex is open to everyone, not just the wealthy or institutional investors. Plus, with the availability of leverage, traders can control larger positions than what their initial capital might suggest, although it's crucial to understand the risks that leverage brings.

An additional advantage is the ability to trade anytime during the workweek. The Forex market spans different time zones across the globe, beginning in Sydney and moving west as the day unfolds. This continuous operation means traders can react instantly to news and events that may affect the market, rather than waiting for an exchange to open. For individuals who work regular day jobs, the ability to trade in the evening or early morning hours aligns nicely with personal commitments.

Furthermore, Forex provides a level of flexibility that other markets simply can't match. Because you're not buying physical assets, but rather speculating on the price movements of currencies, you have the flexibility to go long or short with ease. When you anticipate a currency will strengthen, you buy it (going long), and if you believe it will depreciate, you can sell it (going short). This dual-directional trade capability means profitability can be achieved in both rising and falling markets, promising opportunities no matter the market's condition.

The multitude of trading strategies available in Forex further emphasizes its broad appeal. Many traders find that they can develop a style that suits their personal preferences, risk tolerance, and time commitment. Whether you prefer day trading, swing trading, or position trading, Forex offers room to explore and adapt various strategies. This versatility plays a pivotal role in attracting traders from diverse backgrounds, each looking to carve out their niche.

In addition to strategy flexibility, Forex trading is often seen as a leveling field due to its efficient dissemination of information. Unlike other financial markets where insider information might play a larger role, Forex depends heavily on macroeconomic news and global events, which are equally available to professional and retail traders alike. This democratization of information allows informed traders, regardless of experience level, to have equal standing in taking advantage of market moves.

Another key advantage is the technological advances that have been integrated into Forex trading. Modern trading platforms offer cutting-edge tools and analytics, enabling traders to perform comprehensive technical analysis and execute trades with accuracy and speed. These platforms are designed to be user-friendly, which is particularly beneficial for beginners who are still familiarizing themselves with Forex processes and terminologies.

Risk management tools are another significant advantage that Forex trading presents. Most trading platforms come equipped with customizable alerts and automatic stop-loss functionality, empowering traders to manage risk in a controlled manner. By using these features wisely, traders can protect their investments against undesired market movements. These tools are invaluable for new traders, as they help in learning how to balance risk and reward over time.

Lastly, the global nature of the Forex market means that traders can gain exposure to international economies and political activities. Following global economic events and geopolitical news not only aids traders in making informed decisions but also broadens their understanding of the world's financial landscape. This exposure can lead to both personal and professional growth, offering new perspectives that are invaluable in today's interconnected world.

In conclusion, the numerous advantages that Forex trading offers make it an attractive option for beginners eager to learn and navigate through the financial market. With its high liquidity, low entry barriers, flexibility, advanced technological tools, and accessible information, the Forex market stands as an exhilarating landscape amended only by one's ambition and drive. While challenges exist, adopting a well-rounded understanding of these advantages can lead to profitable pursuits and enriching experiences.

Chapter 2: Currency Pairs Explained

At the heart of Forex trading lies the concept of currency pairs, the building blocks of this massive global market. Imagine two currencies tied together, moving in a synchronized dance based on their relative value. The first currency in the pair, known as the base currency, represents the measure of strength or weakness against the second, referred to as the quote currency. Understanding these pairs is crucial for navigating the Forex market; they dictate how you'll read prices and make your trades. Depending on their composition, currency pairs are categorized into major, minor, and exotic types, each offering unique opportunities and risks. Learning how to interpret these pairs will open the doors to identifying potential trades and building the confidence you need to explore the dynamic world of Forex trading.

Major, Minor, and Exotic Pairs

As you embark on the fascinating journey of Forex trading, understanding the diversity of currency pairs is essential. In Forex trading, currencies are quoted in pairs, which means you're always trading one currency against another. These pairs fall into three main categories: major, minor, and exotic pairs, each with its distinct characteristics and considerations.

Major Currency Pairs are the most traded and liquid pairs in the Forex market. They consist of the currency of the world's largest economies and always include the US dollar (USD) on one side. The most commonly traded major pairs are EUR/USD, USD/JPY, GBP/USD, and USD/CHF. What makes these pairs “major” is not only their global economic relevance but also high trading volume, which leads to tight spreads. This means you’ll typically incur lower transaction costs.

One of the key benefits of trading major pairs lies in their volatility, which, while moderate compared to some minor and exotic pairs, offers ample trading opportunities. Their popularity among traders ensures a wealth of information and analysis available, making it somewhat easier for new traders to find resources and support. Due to their liquidity, major pairs are less prone to manipulation and typically exhibit predictable price movements.

Minor Currency Pairs, on the other hand, consist of pairs that don’t include the US dollar but are made up of other strong economies’ currencies. Examples include EUR/GBP, AUD/JPY, and GBP/CAD. Although they’re less traded compared to major pairs, minors still hold significant value in the market. As a new trader, you might find the minors slightly more challenging due to their typically wider spreads and lower liquidity.

The advantages of trading minor pairs largely relate to the opportunities they provide outside of the major pairs. They offer traders a chance to capitalize on the movements of other strong global economies and allow for portfolio diversification. By understanding the economies behind these currencies, traders can take advantage of specific regional factors and economic indicators that may not affect major pairs.

Exotic Currency Pairs bring a different level of complexity and opportunity to Forex trading. These pairs comprise one major currency paired with the currency of an emerging economy, such as USD/TRY (Turkish Lira) or USD/ZAR (South African Rand). They are considered "exotic" due to the economic fluctuations and political instability that can affect the emerging market currencies involved.

Trading exotic pairs can be enticing due to their potential for significant price movements, but they also entail higher risks. These pairs usually come with much wider spreads, increased volatility, and less available market information. As a novice, approaching exotic pairs requires caution and a well-researched strategy. They're best suited for those who have a deeper understanding of the market dynamics and risk management techniques.

When deciding which type of currency pair to trade, it's important to consider your risk tolerance, trading style, and market knowledge. Major pairs offer stability and predictable patterns, which can be ideal for beginners. Minors present diversification opportunities but require a more comprehensive analysis of their constituent currencies. Exotics, while offering high volatility, demand a robust risk management approach due to their unpredictability and wider spreads.

It's essential to stay informed about global economic developments and geopolitical events, as these factors play a critical role in the fluctuations of currency pairs. For instance, major pairs are often influenced by macroeconomic data from large economies like the US, Eurozone, UK, and Japan, while minor and exotic pairs might be affected by regional economic policies and political instability.

By recognizing the unique characteristics and potential risks associated with major, minor, and exotic pairs, you'll be better equipped to make informed trading decisions. Each type of pair offers various opportunities and challenges, requiring thoughtful analysis and strategy. Whether you aim for stability or seek the thrill of higher volatility, understanding these categories is fundamental to building a successful Forex trading journey. Remember, the Forex market is vast and diverse, and your ability to navigate it with confidence depends on your grasp of these basic building blocks.

Reading a Currency Pair

When venturing into the world of Forex trading, understanding how to read a currency pair is essential. At its core, a currency pair is a simple concept: it's the quotation of two different currencies, with the value of one currency being quoted against the other. The most common structure you'll encounter looks something like this: EUR/USD. This example represents the euro (EUR) versus the U.S. dollar (USD). Reading it is straightforward: the first currency (EUR) is the base currency, and the second one (USD) is the quote currency. Let's break down what this entails.

The base currency is the benchmark in a currency pair. It represents how much of the quote currency is needed to buy one unit of the base currency. So if the EUR/USD is quoted at 1.1500, it means that 1 euro is equivalent to 1.1500 U.S. dollars. This relation is fundamental to understanding how Forex trades work. It shows the direct relationship between the two currencies in question, and it's crucial for calculating trade profits and losses.

Delving deeper, each currency pair is composed of an international currency code standardized by the International Organization for Standardization (ISO). This code consists of three letters, where the first two letters typically identify the country, and the third represents the national currency. For instance, in the USD, 'US' stands for the United States, and 'D' represents the dollar.

One of the alluring aspects of currency pairs is their vast range and versatility. Major pairs include the world's most traded currencies, such as EUR/USD, GBP/USD (British pound/U.S. dollar), and USD/JPY (U.S. dollar/Japanese yen). These are popular due to their high liquidity, which ensures speedy trade execution and typically tighter spreads. Minor pairs exclude the U.S. dollar, like EUR/GBP (euro/British pound) or EUR/AUD (euro/Australian dollar). Exotic pairs involve lesser-known currencies and usually have higher spreads due to their lower liquidity.

Each pair fluctuates constantly due to various factors, including economic reports, geopolitical events, and changes in market sentiment. These fluctuations create opportunities for traders to profit from currency movements. The dynamic nature of these pairs is why understanding how to read them accurately can lead to successful trading strategies.

Certain terms are vital when discussing currency pairs, such as "bid" and "ask". The bid price is what buyers are willing to pay for a currency, while the ask price is what sellers want in exchange for that currency. The difference between these two prices is known as the spread. Spreads can vary significantly depending on the pair and the current market conditions.

Moreover, Forex trading isn't done on a centralized exchange but rather over-the-counter. This setup means currency prices are quoted by different institutions or brokers, and prices might vary slightly from one broker to another. It's crucial for traders to find a reliable source or platform to get the best possible quotation and execution for their trades.

It's also important to discuss the concept of pip—short for "point in percentage." A pip is the smallest price movement in the exchange rate a market can make, based on market convention. For most currency pairs, a pip is a movement in the fourth decimal place, except pairs that include the Japanese yen, where a pip is in the second decimal place. This seemingly small unit is pivotal, as trading decisions often revolve around price changes measured in pips.

Traders need to not only understand these concepts but also translate them into actionable insights. Knowing how to read and analyze currency pairs opens up a landscape of strategic opportunities, allowing a trader to anticipate potential market movements, react to breaking news with precision, and build a resilient portfolio capable of withstanding the market's rollercoaster ride.

Finally, adjustments in global financial conditions can affect currency values profoundly. Interest rates, employment data, and geopolitical stability all play significant roles. By keeping an eye on such indicators, traders can better position themselves to take advantage of shifts in currency dynamics. Forecasting these changes may require a mix of technical and fundamental analysis, but it holds the key to maximizing success in Forex trading.

Chapter 3: Going Long or Short

As you dive deeper into the world of forex trading, understanding the fundamental strategies of going long or short becomes essential; it's the bedrock of tactical decision-making in this dynamic market. When you "go long," you're purchasing a currency pair anticipating that its value will rise so you can sell it later at a profit. Conversely, "going short" involves selling a currency pair with the expectation that its value will drop, allowing you to buy it back at a lower price, thus profiting from the difference. These strategies offer flexibility and broaden your potential for profit, regardless of market direction. Whether the forex market is trending upwards or downwards, knowing when to deploy these strategies can dramatically impact your trading outcomes. Mastery of going long and short isn't just about making trades; it's about cultivating the confidence to anticipate market movements and act decisively, embracing the ebb and flow of forex with foresight and agility. Armed with this knowledge, you'll be better equipped to harness opportunities, navigate risks, and ultimately achieve your trading goals.

The Concept of Buying and Selling in Forex

In the bustling world of Forex trading, grasping the concept of buying and selling is as crucial as understanding the rules of a game. At its core, Forex transactions hinge on the simultaneous buying of one currency and selling of another. This dual-action forms the backbone of every trade in the Forex market, distinguishing it from traditional stock markets. It might seem a bit abstract at first, but let's dive into the mechanics and see how it all fits together.

The process of buying and selling in Forex involves currency pairs, where the first currency listed is known as the base currency, and the second is the quote currency. When you 'go long,' you buy the base currency and sell the quote currency. For instance, if you go long on the EUR/USD pair, you're essentially purchasing euros while selling the equivalent amount of US dollars. You're betting that the euro will increase in value relative to the dollar. Pretty straightforward, right?

Conversely, when you 'go short' in Forex, the transaction is reversed. Here, you sell the base currency while buying the quote currency. In practical terms, going short on EUR/USD means selling euros while buying dollars, speculating that the euro will weaken against the dollar. The beauty of Forex trading lies in this flexibility—providing traders with the opportunity to profit from both upward and downward movements in the currency markets.

Now, let's explore how the Forex market lets traders capitalize on these movements. Unlike traditional stock markets that require physical ownership and delivery of assets, the Forex market operates on margin-based trading. It allows traders to control large positions with a relatively small amount of actual capital. This is a double-edged sword, offering the potential for amplified gains as well as the risk of larger losses. So, understanding the margin requirements set by your broker becomes essential as you strategize on buying and selling decisions.

Additionally, the Forex market operates on a 24-hour basis, offering ample opportunities to contemplate trades at your convenience, no matter the time zone you're in. This around-the-clock market structure supports various trading strategies and styles, from day trading to long-term investment approaches. The choice of when to enter and exit trades varies widely among individual traders, based on their specific goals and market analysis.

When deciding to go long or short, it's crucial to acknowledge the factors influencing currency values. Economic indicators, geopolitical events, and market sentiments are just a few elements that impact currency fluctuations. Successful traders learn to interpret and anticipate these dynamics, incorporating them into their buying and selling decisions. This highlights the importance of incorporating fundamental and technical analysis into your trading strategies—topics that we'll discuss in depth in upcoming chapters.

Furthermore, Forex trading demands a deep understanding of order types. Market orders, limit orders, and stop-loss orders are among the tools in a trader's arsenal. Each order type serves a unique purpose, offering flexibility and control over your trades. Whether you're aiming to enter the market at a specific price point or looking to safeguard your investments against adverse market moves, selecting the right type of order is essential.

As with any financial market, the ultimate goal in Forex trading is to act on your predictions of price movement to secure a profit. Enthusiastic traders often enter positions quickly, only to realize that a thorough evaluation of potential outcomes is fundamental. It's about choosing the right moments to take action—timing is a cornerstone of successful Forex trading.

Since Forex involves high stakes, a well-rounded trading plan becomes indispensable. This plan should encompass entry and exit strategies, risk management parameters, and a disciplined approach to trading. It's not just about knowing when to buy or sell; it's about preparing for various market scenarios and making informed decisions. In later chapters, we'll build on this foundation by exploring how you can craft a sturdy trading plan tailored to your unique objectives in the Forex landscape.

Ultimately, maneuvering through the Forex market by going long or short is a dynamic and engaging endeavor. It invites traders to hone their skills, sharpen their instincts, and, most importantly, learn continuously. With dedication and practice, the concept of buying and selling in Forex transforms from an abstract idea into a powerful tool for potential success in this thrilling global market.

The Mechanics of Executing Trades

When you're dipping your toes into the Forex market, understanding the mechanics of executing trades is essential to laying a solid foundation. Forex trading, essentially the act of buying and selling currencies, requires knowledge of both the logistical processes and the theoretical concepts that drive your decisions. This section will guide you through executing Forex trades efficiently, providing insights into ensuring those trades align with your market expectations.

To start, let's explore the basic setup of a trade. In Forex, you're constantly working with pairs of currencies. You'll essentially determine whether one currency will strengthen or weaken against the other. Suppose you're banking on the value of the Euro climbing against the US Dollar. In that case, you'd execute a "buy" order for the EUR/USD pair, which translates to going long. Conversely, expecting the Euro to fall, you'd execute a "sell" order, indicating a short position. This is where the understanding of 'going long or short' becomes practical and real-time.

Before diving into a trade, it's vital to decide on specific parameters such as the entry point, the amount you want to trade, stop-loss levels, and take-profit thresholds. These parameters aren't just numbers but define your approach to managing risk and ensuring profitability. Every successful trader knows the importance of setting these boundaries; they serve as your safety net and enable clarity of thought during market volatility. It's not simply about pulling the trigger on a trade; it's about orchestrating your strategy with precision.

Once your parameters are set, choosing the right Forex trading platform is paramount. Most platforms offer straightforward processes to place trades, but becoming familiar with the interface can significantly affect your efficiency and effectiveness. On the trading platform, you'll see the currency pair's chart, which displays its real-time value, and buttons to execute buy or sell actions based on your prepared strategy. Accuracy is critical here—mistakes can be costly.

Now, let's discuss order types. The most common are market orders, limit orders, and stop orders. A market order is executed immediately at the current market price, while a limit order enables you to buy or sell at a predetermined price. A stop order, on the other hand, becomes a market order when it's activated at your price point. Understanding these order types puts decision-making power in your hands, allowing you to adapt your trades to market conditions efficiently.

The execution process involves communicating with your broker—the intermediary facilitating your trades. Choosing a broker who meets your needs is fundamental to smooth trading mechanics. For instance, your broker can influence the speed of trade executions, and transaction costs, and even provide educational resources that can aid in improving your strategies.

Speed is of the essence in Forex trading. The market operates 24 hours a day across different time zones, which affects liquidity and volatility. Faster execution reduces the slippage, a gap between the expected price of a trade and the price at which the trade is actually executed, that can affect profitability. With more advanced trading platforms and technologies, you now have access to near-instantaneous trade execution which was once reserved for institutional investors.

Margins also play a crucial role in the execution of trades. They allow traders to leverage their trading positions, increasing potential returns. Understanding how much margin is required for a trade and how that impacts your account's available equity is vital. Utilizing leverage responsibly ensures that while potential profits can be maximized, potential losses do not wipe out your capital. This careful balance is what separates successful Forex traders from novices.

Continuous monitoring of your trades after execution is just as important as the initial setup. Forex trading isn't static, and like the markets themselves, your strategies need to be dynamic. Adjusting your stop-loss or take-profit levels can further secure your investments or capitalize on market movements. Whether you're constantly checking your trades or using automated trading systems, maintaining oversight is key.

Automated trading systems and algorithms have become increasingly popular as they can execute trades on your behalf based on predefined criteria, removing the human emotion factor from decision-making. While these systems can offer efficiency, they also require careful calibration and a deep understanding of the trading signals they react to.

The mechanics of executing trades also encompass the crucial aspect of timing. Entering and exiting trades at the right moment can be the difference between a profit and a loss. This requires not only an acute awareness of the market and its signals but also the patience and discipline to wait for the right setup. Whether following technical analysis, market news, or instinct, aligning timing with strategy can leverage trade execution success.

Finally, reflecting on each executed trade—whether it resulted in profit or loss—serves as a learning experience that sharpens future strategies. The Forex market is ever-evolving, and staying informed with new techniques, economic conditions, and technological advancements is crucial. By evaluating your trades and understanding the mechanics behind each action, you become better equipped to refine your methodology and enhance your successes over time.

Chapter 4: Calculating Pips and Points

As we delve deeper into the mechanics of forex trading, understanding how to calculate pips and points becomes essential. Think of a pip as the tiny measurement that indicates the change in value between two currencies—a cornerstone concept. This minuscule movement can unlock vast potential, giving you a quantifiable measure of market fluctuations. The standard pip value is usually the fourth decimal place in most currency pairs, though exceptions like the Japanese yen currency pairs use the second decimal. Calculating pip value is where the math meets strategy, as it directly ties into your profit and risk management practices. A savvy trader knows the importance of mastering this, not as a chore but as an empowering tool to navigate the turbulent waters of forex markets. Seeing these small shifts allows you to make knowledgeable and informed predictions, strengthening your confidence in each trade you make. Understanding and calculating pips and points might seem like a meticulous task, yet it's the starting point for crafting profitable trades. Remember, every great trader started with just a pip.

What Is a Pip?

In the expansive realm of Forex trading, mastering certain fundamental concepts is crucial to unlocking a trader's potential. One of the cornerstones of this knowledge is understanding what a pip is, as it forms the basis for calculating profits, losses, and price movements in the market. Let's delve into the world of pips and discover why they're so essential.

A "pip," which stands for "percentage in point," is a unit of measurement that expresses the change in value between two currencies in a currency pair. Essentially, a pip is the smallest price move that an exchange rate can make, based on market convention. For the majority of currency pairs, a pip is 0.0001, which is the fourth decimal place. But why is this tiny change so important?

Consider trading the EUR/USD currency pair. If the exchange rate moves from 1.1000 to 1.1001, this 0.0001 movement represents a one pip shift. While this fraction might seem minor or even negligible, in the world of Forex trading, even the smallest fluctuation can significantly affect the outcome of a trade, especially when leveraging larger sums of money.

To further illustrate the importance of a pip, think of it as the gauge of a winning or losing trade. Traders use pips as a standardized measure, allowing them to communicate their results and strategies effectively. For instance, saying that a trade earned 100 pips conveys clear information regarding the scope of profit, irrespective of the currency pair involved.

However, it's crucial to note that not all currency pairs measure a pip this way. For example, currency pairs involving the Japanese yen, such as USD/JPY, have a pip value at the second decimal place (0.01). Therefore, if the USD/JPY moves from 110.00 to 110.01, that's considered a one pip change. These exceptions illustrate the diverse and nuanced nature of Forex trading, reinforcing the importance of grasping the basics thoroughly.

Understanding what a pip is holds significant practical value for traders. It enables them to set stop-loss levels, define take-profit points, and adequately gauge the potential risks and rewards of a trade. In conclusion, a pip isn't just a trivial fraction; it's a trader's link to market dynamics and the essential currency of Forex trading success. As we move forward with this knowledge, remember that every pip counts, and mastering this insight is a step closer to becoming a proficient Forex trader.

How to Calculate Pip Value

When you venture into the realm of Forex trading, understanding how to calculate pip value is fundamental. This calculation not only helps you manage risk but also gives clarity on potential profitability or losses in your trades. Pip value, simply put, is the monetary value attributed to a one-pip change in the exchange rate. For the uninitiated, a pip is typically the smallest movement that currency pairs can make, often calculated in five decimal places but commonly discussed up to the fourth decimal place for major currency pairs. The fourth decimal place is what most Forex traders refer to as a pip. Moreover, comprehending pip values is essential as it directly influences your trading decisions and financial strategies.

To begin, remember that pip value calculations differ depending on the base currency in a given currency pair and your account's currency. For instance, if your account is denominated in U.S. dollars and you're trading a currency pair where the USD is the quote currency, like EUR/USD, the pip value is straightforward. Typically, for a standard lot size of 100,000 units of the base currency, every one-pip movement equates to $10. A mini lot of 10,000 units corresponds to $1 per pip, while a micro lot of 1,000 units translates to $0.10 per pip. These simple rules give traders a baseline for estimating how exchange rate fluctuations affect their positions.

Now, let's discuss cases where the U.S. dollar isn't the quote currency. Here's where some calculations kick in. When USD is the base currency, as with USD/JPY, the pip value formula takes a slightly different path. If we assume you're trading a standard lot, the calculation for pip value is based on the actual exchange rate. First, take the size of the lot, typically 100,000, and multiply it by one pip, such as 0.01 for JPY or 0.0001 for others, and then divide by the current exchange rate. This formula gives you the pip value in your local currency. For example, if USD/JPY is at 110.00, the pip value for a standard lot would be approximately $9.09.

Another intriguing scenario arises when the currency pair doesn't involve U.S. dollars at all, known as a cross-currency pair like EUR/GBP. Here, determining the pip value gets slightly more complex, as it involves calculating the value in USD before translating it back into your account currency. Essentially, you'll use the standard lot method, multiply by one pip, and then convert the resulting amount using either the exchange rate provided by your broker or the rate at which the trade is conducted. Such conversions might seem daunting initially, but they are invaluable for understanding financial outcomes.

For traders working with currency pairs such as GBP/JPY, where neither currency is USD, pip value calculation involves additional steps. As an example, for a standard lot with a pair like GBP/JPY at an exchange rate of 150.00, the formula takes on an extra conversion step. After calculating the pip value like a JPY pair, you'll convert it using the current exchange rate between USD and the base currency, GBP in this case. These layers of calculation ensure precise risk management and enable traders to execute informed strategies.

Technology assists significantly in simplifying pip value calculations. Most trading platforms incorporate this functionality, offering traders the convenience of instant calculations during trade execution. These platforms typically automatically compute pip values for every trade, based on real-time exchange rates and current market conditions. Utilizing these tools can provide real-time insight and help develop consistently profitable trading habits.

Grasping pip value serves as a cornerstone for other critical aspects of Forex trading, such as setting stop-loss and take-profit levels. Both these concepts hinge on accurate pip calculations, impacting how much you're willing to risk versus how much you're expecting to gain. Ensuring these levels align with your pip understanding can lead to more disciplined and potentially fruitful trading practices.

Let's not overlook the influence of leverage in pip value calculations and trading risks. With leverage, a small change in pip value can lead to significant shifts in your trading outcomes. While leverage makes Forex trading more accessible by allowing you to control larger positions with less capital, it also amplifies both profits and losses. Traders should be attuned to how pip values interact with leverage to avoid undue exposure and ensure sustainable trading practices.

Seasoned traders often use spreadsheets or leverage advanced trading software to keep track of pip value changes and evaluate their impact comprehensively. While this can seem intricate for newcomers, cultivating this level of rigour in your trading approach pays dividends in reducing errors and optimizing your transactions. As you gain experience, maintaining meticulous records will help improve strategies and adaptation in fluctuating market conditions.

In sum, mastering the calculation of pip value is a foundational skill in Forex trading. It doesn't just underpin effective financial management but acts as a stepping stone to more advanced trading practices. By integrating this knowledge with other trading insights, you empower yourself to navigate the Forex market's complexities and craft strategies grounded in sound analysis. Embrace this mastery, and see how it shapes your ability to make informed, confident decisions in the world of currency trading.

Chapter 5: Leverage and Margin in Forex

In Forex trading, leverage and margin are powerful tools that can significantly amplify both potential profits and risks. By using leverage, traders can control a larger position with a relatively small amount of capital, enabling them to maximize the efficiency of their investment. However, this enlarged capacity to trade comes with increased risk, as both losses and gains are magnified. It's crucial for new traders to grasp how leverage affects their trading, not only in terms of potential outcomes but also in understanding margin requirements that brokers demand to secure these trades. Margin acts as a deposit to ensure you can cover potential losses, and knowing how to calculate requisite margins can prevent unintended surprises and maintain your trading account in good standing. Mastering leverage and margin is like holding the key to navigating the Forex market confidently, enabling you to make informed decisions while safeguarding your investments against unforeseen market fluctuations.

Understanding Leverage

Leverage in forex trading is like a magic tool that can amplify your trading power, allowing you to control a larger position with a relatively small amount of your own capital. Imagine you're a small-time prospector with the opportunity to control a much larger chunk of the gold mine than you could afford on your own. That's leverage. In forex, brokers provide this boost, and while it can enhance your potential profits, it also magnifies your risks. This means decisions need to be thoughtful and calculated. As you explore leverage, recognize it as a double-edged sword, capable of rapidly transforming your fortunes but also requiring diligent risk management. Your journey into the forex world becomes more dynamic as you harness leverage, turning the potential of minor investments into significant opportunities.

How Leverage Affects Trading In the world of Forex, understanding how leverage works and how it affects trading is crucial. Leverage is like a double-edged sword; it can amplify your profits, but it can just as easily magnify your losses. This characteristic makes leverage a powerful tool, but it also demands respect and careful management.

So, let's break it down. Leverage allows you to control a large position in the Forex market with a relatively small amount of your own money. This means, for instance, with a leverage ratio of 100:1, you could control $10,000 in the market with just $100 of your own funds. It's about using borrowed capital to enhance potential returns, and similarly, potential risks.

At first glance, leverage may seem like a fantastic opportunity. Who wouldn't want the chance to increase their potential returns with less initial investment? Yet, it's essential to remember that while leverage can boost wins, it can also amplify losses. This amplification can sometimes catch new traders by surprise if they haven't fully grasped the consequences.

In practical terms, leverage affects your trading strategy's outcomes significantly. When your account is leveraged, even small price movements in the wrong direction can lead to substantial losses. This is why risk management strategies, such as setting stop-loss orders, are invaluable tools to protect your trading capital. Knowing when to cut losses is as vital as letting profits run.

Moreover, leverage requires a trader to be more vigilant about market fluctuations and their account balance. Many successful Forex traders understand that using appropriate leverage levels consistent with their risk tolerance and trading plan is key to sustainable trading. Excessive leverage can lead to margin calls, where your broker requires you to deposit more funds or close positions to cover potential losses.

The psychological impact of trading with leverage shouldn't be underestimated either. The pressure of knowing that both potential gains and losses are magnified can affect decision-making abilities. It's crucial to have emotional discipline and a clear plan to avoid rash decisions fueled by emotion rather than sound strategy.

As you navigate the Forex market, recognizing leverage's role in your trading outcomes will help you develop more effective strategies. By setting sensible limits on leverage usage, you not only minimize risk but also increase your odds of maintaining a balanced trading account over time.

Understanding the impact of leverage involves more than just knowing the mechanics; it means integrating that knowledge into your overall trading approach. An informed trader recognizes when to employ leverage and when to scale back, considering current market conditions and their personal trading objectives.

Finally, remember that leverage is a tool, much like any indicator or piece of market information. Used wisely, it can enhance your trading capabilities. However, misused, it can lead to significant losses. Education and a well-thought-out strategy will help ensure that leverage serves as an asset rather than a liability in your trading journey.

Understanding Margin

Margin in Forex trading is like the key that unlocks leverage, allowing you to control a larger position with a relatively small amount of your own money. Think of it as a sort of security deposit held by your broker to ensure you can cover potential losses. It's crucial to understand that while margin can amplify your gains, it can just as easily magnify your losses. This requires you to manage it wisely to avoid margin calls, which occur when your account balance falls below the required level set by your broker. Margin is calculated based on the trade size and leverage ratio, making it vital for traders to comprehend how these elements interact. Mastering margin means not just knowing how much you need to trade, but also strategically managing your risk, ensuring that you're trading in a way that's both responsible and empowering. This knowledge will help you make informed decisions, maintaining control over your trades rather than being dictated by the market's often unpredictable nature. By keeping a firm grip on how margin works, you're better equipped to navigate the Forex market with confidence and precision.

Margin Requirements and Calculations are fundamental concepts you'd encounter early in your Forex trading journey. To understand them, you need to first grasp the basics of margin itself. Simply put, margin is a portion of your funds that a broker sets aside when you open a leveraged position. It's like a security deposit, ensuring that you can cover potential losses. But how does one figure out the exact margin requirement for a trade? Let's break it down together, as it's a crucial part of prudent Forex trading.

To calculate margin requirements, brokers usually express this amount as a percentage of the full position value. For instance, a common margin level might be 1% or 2%. If you're interested in trading a currency contract worth $100,000, you'll need to have $1,000 or $2,000 as margin, depending on the margin percentage. It's that simple! This means you're essentially controlling a $100,000 position with a much smaller financial commitment. The beauty here? You can wield substantial buying power with relatively minimal capital.

However, there's more to these figures than meets the eye. Margin requirements vary not just by broker, but also by the currency pair and market conditions. So, when volatility spikes, brokers might adjust their margin requirements to mitigate risk. It's essential to stay informed and aware of any changes that occur. Savvy traders anticipate and prepare for these shifts, ensuring they're not caught off guard.

Another key calculation involves understanding the concept of "free margin", which is the money available in your account that isn't tied up in existing trades. It's crucial to monitor your free margin because it influences your ability to open new trades and withstand market movements. If your equity falls due to adverse market changes, your free margin decreases, potentially impacting your ability to maintain open positions. Nobody wants that nasty surprise of a margin call.

Speaking of margin calls, these occur when your account equity falls below the required margin level. It's a broker's way of nudging you to add more funds or to close some positions. Understanding how to calculate the equity in your account against the used margin can help you steer clear of these unwanted notifications. Precision in your calculations keeps the dreaded margin call at bay.

Let's use an example to see how margin requirements and calculations impact your trading. Imagine you're trading a mini lot (10,000 units of currency) in the EUR/USD pair with a 2% margin requirement. If the exchange rate is 1.2000, the notional value of your trade is $12,000. With a 2% margin requirement, you'd need $240 as margin in your account. This calculation balances the power of leverage with the risk control of margin, empowering you to make strategic decisions on capital allocation.

Additionally, keeping an eye on the "margin level" percentage can serve as an early warning system. This percentage is calculated by dividing your account equity by the used margin and multiplying by

100. A margin level above 100% indicates room for maneuverability, while dipping below this threshold might put you in the danger zone of a margin call. Equipping yourself with these calculation skills can make navigating volatile markets less daunting.

Importantly, as you build your trading knowledge, understanding margin requirements doesn't just end at numbers. It transforms into a mindset. You find peace in knowing that with every trade, you've measured your risk down to a decimal. You're not just aiming for profitability but striving toward a sustainable trading journey. Embrace the intelligence that's inherent in margin calculations; it's your ally.

Margin requirements and calculations are your training wheels, allowing you to make mistakes safely as you learn. They give you the opportunity to fine-tune your strategies, and take bold steps with a well-calculated safety net. As you grow more confident with this, remember you're positioning yourself for greater opportunities. You've got this!

In conclusion, understanding and calculating margin requirements is more than just number crunching. It's cultivating a solid framework to support your decision-making process throughout your trades. Every calculation sharpens your instinct and builds a portfolio of skills that guides you in times of uncertainty. So let's leverage this knowledge, literally and metaphorically, to embark on successful Forex trading endeavors.

Chapter 6: Analyzing the Forex Market

Diving into the world of Forex analysis provides traders a vital edge. In this chapter, we journey through the nuanced realms of fundamental and technical analysis, equipping you with the tools needed to make informed decisions. By understanding economic indicators and events, you begin to see how geopolitical factors can sway currency values. Technical analysis, on the other hand, delves into chart patterns and indicators, helping you predict market movements with greater confidence. Whether you're examining a country's GDP or evaluating candlestick formations, analyzing the Forex market requires both a keen eye and a holistic approach. Mastering these analyses can transform you from a beginner to a strategist, ready to tackle the ever-evolving Forex landscape. As you continue reading, remember that practice transforms theory into skill, positioning you to seize opportunities in the grand tapestry of global finance.

Fundamental Analysis

Fundamental analysis is all about understanding the bigger picture that drives currency value changes in the Forex market. For beginners, it's like peeking under the hood of an economy to see what really makes it tick. This involves analyzing economic indicators such as GDP growth, unemployment rates, and interest rates—which serve as the pulse of a nation's economic health. By examining major news events and financial reports, traders learn to anticipate market movements before they happen. It's a bit like being a detective, piecing together economic clues to predict future currency trends. Fundamentally-driven insights help traders grasp why currencies move in particular ways—and that insight is power. Whether it's the ripple of a central bank's interest rate decision or a government's fiscal policy shift, these factors can trigger market volatility, opening up opportunities for those ready to take the plunge. Understanding these elements gives beginners the confidence to make calculated decisions, ultimately turning their analysis into profit.

Economic Indicators and Events form the backbone of fundamental analysis in the Forex market. Fundamental analysis is all about understanding the economic forces that cause currency values to fluctuate. It's a discipline that requires an in-depth look at global economies, and key among the tools used are economic indicators and events that can signal opportunities for traders.

Economic indicators are quantifiable pieces of data or statistics that shed light on the economic performance of a country or region. These indicators range from employment figures and inflation rates to GDP growth numbers and retail sales statistics. Each indicator provides unique insights into different facets of an economy, influencing investor confidence and subsequently affecting currency flows.

One of the most significant economic events is the release of employment data, especially figures like the U.S. Non-Farm Payrolls. This report is released monthly and measures employment changes, providing an indicator of economic health. A higher-than-expected payroll figure usually indicates a strengthening economy, boosting the U.S. dollar, while a lower figure might weaken the currency.

Inflation metrics, such as the Consumer Price Index (CPI) and the Producer Price Index (PPI), are vital as they reflect the purchasing power of consumers. Higher inflation typically pushes central banks to raise interest rates, increasing currency value. On the other hand, lower inflation might lead to rate cuts, devaluing the currency. Understanding these dynamics can offer traders a fair idea of how currency pairs might move in the future.

Gross Domestic Product (GDP) is another critical indicator. It reflects the total economic output of a country. A robust GDP growth signals a healthy, expanding economy, which tends to strengthen the national currency as it attracts foreign investments. Conversely, a low GDP might discourage such investments, weakening the currency.

In addition to regular indicator reports, unexpected economic events can cause significant swings in currency prices. These include geopolitical events, natural disasters, or abrupt policy changes. For instance, an unexpected interest rate hike by a central bank can cause immediate currency appreciation as investors rush to benefit from higher yields. Strategic forex trading involves keeping a pulse on such potential events to preemptively adjust trading positions.

Central bank meetings and monetary policy statements also play a central role in shaping currency movements. Traders pay close attention to these events, analyzing central bank policies, outlooks, and rate decisions. Forward guidance, which refers to central bank projections on future policy, provides a window into possible future rate adjustments, influencing market sentiments and currency valuations.

Increasing one's awareness of these indicators and events isn't merely about data collection—it's about interpreting these signals and understanding their implications. For instance, a trader might note that the European Central Bank plans to maintain low rates to drive growth and adjust their euro exposure accordingly. Staying proactive in interpreting such data ensures traders are not just reacting to the market but anticipating movements.

One might wonder, how often should traders monitor these indicators? Successful forex trading doesn't equate to staying glued to news constantly but rather understanding the economic calendar. Key dates on this calendar, especially when major economies release data, should be essential periods where traders reassess their strategies and align them with the potential market impacts.

This knowledge about economic indicators doesn't function in isolation. Traders should integrate this understanding with other analytical tools for a comprehensive approach. Technical analysis often complements fundamental insights, enabling traders to validate their positions with concrete chart data and trends.

However, remember that economic indicators can often present conflicting signals. For instance, strong GDP growth might coincide with rising inflation, prompting a complex scenario where currencies could either appreciate due to growth or decline over inflation fears. Navigating such complexities requires skill and a nuanced understanding of the global economic landscape.

Ultimately, mastering the art of interpreting economic indicators and events not only aids in successful trading but also fosters a broader understanding of global economic dynamics. This knowledge equips traders with the confidence to navigate the forex markets with a strategic mindset, ready to adapt to the ever-changing economic tides that influence currency valuations.

Technical Analysis

To really get a handle on the Forex market, technical analysis becomes your compass. This analytical approach digs into historical price data to project future market movements, offering you a clearer picture of where the market might be heading. By using a blend of chart patterns and technical indicators, you'll learn to decipher price behavior and identify potential trends or reversals. It's like solving a puzzle; you gather pieces of data, fit them together, and form a coherent picture. With tools like moving averages or Fibonacci retracement, you'll build a deeper understanding of market dynamics. Mastering this technique empowers you to make informed, strategic trades based on objective data rather than emotions, ensuring you stay ahead of the game. Ultimately, technical analysis becomes a vital part of your toolkit, helping you turn complexity into clarity in the ever-evolving Forex landscape.

Chart Patterns and Indicators play a crucial role in technical analysis, serving as the compass that guides a trader through the complex world of the Forex market. Understanding these chart patterns and indicators isn't just about knowing what they are; it's about learning how to read the story they tell. This story, which unfolds through patterns on price charts and signals from indicators, helps traders anticipate future price movements, enabling them to make informed trading decisions.

At the heart of chart patterns are the visual formations that represent price movements over a specific period. These formations, such as head and shoulders, flags, triangles, and double tops or bottoms, are more than just shapes; they reflect market psychology and the battle between supply and demand. Each pattern provides traders with clues about potential market reversals or continuations. For instance, a head and shoulders pattern might signal a market reversal, indicating that a trend is about to change direction. The beauty of these patterns lies in their ability to summarize a wealth of information into an easily recognizable form.

Indicators, on the other hand, are mathematical calculations that are based on historical price, volume, or open interest data. These tools, including moving averages, the relative strength index (RSI), and the moving average convergence divergence (MACD), provide additional insights by highlighting certain aspects of the price data that might not be immediately apparent from the chart alone. Indicators can help traders confirm trends, measure market momentum, identify overbought or oversold conditions, and even spot divergences that might suggest an impending reversal.

Incorporating chart patterns and indicators into your trading strategy requires a balance. Patterns often offer the initial signal of potential price action, while indicators serve to confirm or disprove these signals. For example, if a trader spots an ascending triangle pattern—a continuation pattern suggesting further price movement in the current trend direction—they might look at the RSI to confirm that the market isn't overbought or oversold before acting on the signal. This combination ensures that decisions are based on both visual and quantitative data, reducing the likelihood of being misled by noise in the market.

Understanding chart patterns and indicators also involves a deep dive into the psychology of market participants. Patterns emerge as traders collectively make decisions based on a wide array of factors, including economic data, geopolitical events, and sentiment shifts. Recognizing these patterns is akin to reading the pulse of the market. Similarly, indicators often reflect changes in underlying market conditions that may not be captured by patterns alone, such as shifts in momentum or the strength of a trend.

One of the key challenges for new traders is identifying which patterns and indicators are most relevant for their trading style and goals. The array of available options can be overwhelming, but it's important to start with the basics. Moving averages, for instance, are among the simplest yet most effective indicators, helping traders identify the direction of the trend and potential support or resistance levels. As traders gain more experience and confidence, they can explore more complex patterns and indicators, such as Fibonacci retracements or Bollinger Bands.

It's also critical to understand that no pattern or indicator is foolproof. The Forex market is dynamic and unpredictable, influenced by countless variables that can shift sentiment and price direction in an instant. Patterns may fail, and indicators can give false signals. Therefore, risk management is an essential part of using chart patterns and indicators effectively, ensuring that any potential losses are minimized while allowing gains to run. Combining technical analysis with other forms of analysis, such as fundamental analysis, can also provide a more holistic view of the market and its potential directions.

Furthermore, the advent of technology and algorithmic trading has led to the development of computerized trading systems that rely heavily on patterns and indicators. These systems take the guesswork out of the equation, allowing traders to automate their strategies based on predefined conditions. This can be particularly advantageous for those new to Forex trading, as it helps remove emotional bias and ensures consistent execution of trades. However, it's important to approach such systems with caution, ensuring they are thoroughly tested and tailored to your specific trading strategy.

In essence, chart patterns and indicators offer traders a roadmap to navigating the complexities of the Forex market. They provide clarity and direction while helping traders assess the probable direction of price movements. As you embark on your journey into Forex trading, take the time to study these patterns and indicators, practice identifying them on charts, and understand how they align with your overall trading strategy. Doing so will empower you to approach the market with greater confidence and insight, transforming uncertainties into opportunities.

Chapter 7: Risk Management Strategies

As you embark on your Forex trading journey, honing your risk management skills is vital to ensure long-term success and sustainability. The market can be unpredictable, and even seasoned traders face losses, but by implementing smart strategies, you can protect your investments and maximize profits. Start by setting stop-loss and take-profit orders for every trade; this acts as your safety net against unexpected market movements. Managing your trading capital prudently is crucial—avoid overexposure by risking only a small percentage of your account on each trade. Leverage, while powerful, must be used with caution; it can amplify both gains and losses. Remember, embracing risk management is not just about avoiding losses—it's about making informed decisions that allow you to trade with confidence, refine your skills, and ultimately reach your trading goals. By developing a disciplined approach to risk, you're laying a solid foundation for a successful trading career.

Setting Stop-Loss and Take-Profit Orders

In the exhilarating yet risky world of forex trading, mastering the art of setting stop-loss and take-profit orders is crucial. These tools are not just techniques; they're the backbone of a sound risk management strategy. They serve as the safety nets and goalposts for your trades, allowing you to navigate the volatile seas of the forex market with confidence. So, let's dive deep into the mechanics and the mindset needed to wield these powerful instruments effectively.

To start, it's essential to grasp what stop-loss and take-profit orders are. A stop-loss order is a predetermined point at which you'll exit a losing trade to prevent further loss. Think of it as a financial airbag that protects your account from disastrous drawdowns. On the other hand, a take-profit order specifies the price at which you'll close a winning trade to lock in profits. It helps curb the temptation to let a winner run until it reverses and wipes out gains. Setting these orders appropriately involves more than just numerical targets; it requires a nuanced understanding of your risk tolerance and trading objectives.

The beauty of stop-loss and take-profit orders lies in their ability to remove emotion from trading decisions. The forex market is fast-paced and fraught with emotional pitfalls like fear and greed. By pre-setting your exit points, you neutralize these emotions, adhering to a disciplined approach instead. This discipline is paramount when volatile market movements tempt you to rethink your strategies. The discipline of sticking to predetermined points ensures that your decisions are based on strategy, not on the whims of the moment.

Crafting effective stop-loss levels demands a blend of technical analysis and a keen understanding of market dynamics. You should place your stop-loss order at a logical point, such as a well-defined support or resistance level. This tactical approach combines the safeguarding of your trades with a respect for market variability. Placing it too narrowly may lead to premature stop-outs, while a stop-loss too far may expose you to excessive risk. It's all about finding that sweet spot that aligns with your strategy.

Similarly, setting take-profit levels also requires thoughtful consideration. Some traders employ the risk-reward ratio concept to determine these levels, aiming for a ratio that aligns with their overall trading goals. For instance, a trader may set a take-profit order at a level that is twice the distance of the stop-loss. This approach not only encapsulates the potential gains but also helps maintain a healthy balance between risk and reward. Ultimately, a crafted plan combining both stop-loss and take-profit aims to ensure that your trading plan doesn't become a roulette wheel where outcomes are left to chance.

In trading, adaptability cannot be overstated. The market is a living entity, and a rigid approach might not always work. While setting initial stop-loss and take-profit orders is vital, monitoring their appropriateness as the trade unfolds is equally crucial. Markets can change in response to geopolitical events or economic indicators, necessitating adjustments in your strategy. Keeping an eye on such developments allows you to tweak your orders, optimizing them based on new data while avoiding reactionary changes in panic.

Leveraging automation through your trading platform can further enhance the effectiveness of stop-loss and take-profit orders. Modern trading platforms come equipped with features that allow these orders to execute even when you're not glued to your screen. This capability is a boon for traders unable to dedicate full-time attention to the market. It ensures you're covered even during unexpected market swings, keeping your strategy on track regardless of your availability.

Let's not forget that while these orders serve as crucial components of risk management, they should be part of a more holistic strategy. These tools work best when integrated into a broader picture that includes sound money management practices. For instance, ensuring you're not risking more than a small percentage of your total capital on any single trade is a prudent rule to live by. This broad approach reduces the psychological burden of losing trades and expands your runway in the trading landscape.

For beginners, setting stop-loss and take-profit orders might seem daunting, but practice leads to proficiency. Many platforms offer demo accounts where novices can experiment without financial consequences. Engaging in simulated trading helps build the confidence needed to execute these strategies effectively when real money's at stake. Remember, the objective is to transform these concepts into habits that guide decision-making, even under pressure.

Ultimately, setting stop-loss and take-profit orders is an art shaped by continuous learning and experience. Over time, traders learn to trust their analyses, intuition, and strategic planning in establishing these orders. They become a dynamic part of your trading arsenal, responding to both predictable trends and sudden shifts. As you integrate these tools into your trading routine, you'll not only bolster your risk management strategy but also enhance your overall trading acumen. In forex trading, knowledge is power and using stop-loss and take-profit orders wisely is your shield.

Managing Your Trading Capital

One of the fundamental aspects of successful Forex trading is effectively managing your trading capital. This process involves understanding how much of your capital should be at risk on any given trade, as well as implementing strategies to preserve your funds over the long term. It's not just about making money; it's about making sure that your trading account survives for the long haul. Without proper capital management, even the most skilled traders can find themselves out of the market quickly due to string of losses that deplete their accounts.

To start, it's crucial to determine your risk tolerance. This involves assessing how much of your trading capital you are comfortable risking on a single trade. A common rule of thumb among traders is the 1-2% rule, where only 1-2% of your trading capital is at risk in any single trade. This allows you to survive bad trades and remain in the game. It's key to remember that every trade involves risk, so spreading your risk across various trades can help mitigate losses.

Consider diversification, which may seem like a strategy reserved for investment portfolios but is equally relevant in Forex trading. By spreading investments across different currency pairs, you can reduce the risk of significant losses. Diversification does not eliminate risk entirely, but it can reduce the impact of negative movements in one part of your portfolio by offsetting them with gains in another.

Your trading strategy should also include defining your position size. The size of each trade plays a significant role in how much of your capital is at risk. Calculating the appropriate position size involves several factors, including your account balance, risk percentage, and the distance to your stop-loss point. This calculation ensures that you're not over-leveraging or over-exposing your account to risk, which can lead to substantial losses.

One crucial element of managing your trading capital effectively is maintaining a balanced approach to leverage. Leverage can magnify both gains and losses, so using it responsibly is essential. Always consider potential losses when leveraging trades. Many new traders are lured by high leverage without considering the risks involved, leading to rapid depletion of their trading capital.

Part of managing your capital is setting up a reliable record-keeping system. Documenting each trade, including the strategy used, the reasoning behind the trade, the stop-loss and take-profit points, and the outcome, provides invaluable insights. Regularly reviewing your trading journal helps in identifying patterns in your trading behavior and decision-making, which can then be fine-tuned for better outcomes.

Psychological discipline is as crucial in managing trading capital as any technical strategy. Traders often experience emotional highs when trades go well and devastating lows when they don't. It's important to stick to your capital management plan and not allow emotions to dictate your trades. This discipline helps prevent the common pitfall of chasing losses by increasing trade sizes or taking excessively risky positions.

In addition to these strategies, continuously educating yourself and staying informed about market conditions can aid in effective capital management. As market dynamics shift, adapting your risk management strategies to these changes can help preserve your trading capital. This requires a commitment to learning and staying updated with market news and trends, enabling you to make informed decisions based on current events

Lastly, automation and the use of technology can play a role in managing your trading capital. Many trading platforms offer tools that can automatically manage trades for you, setting stop-loss orders, trailing stops, and take-profit levels, according to pre-defined criteria. Utilizing these tools can help remove emotion-driven mistakes from your trading process, allowing for a more consistent and disciplined approach.

Ultimately, managing your trading capital is about taking a balanced, disciplined, and strategic approach to every trade you make. It's about understanding your personal risk tolerance, implementing strategies to preserve your capital, and continually learning to adapt your approach as the market evolves. With this foundation, you can build the confidence needed to trade successfully in the Forex market over the long term.

Using Leverage Safely

Leverage in Forex trading is a powerful tool that lets traders amplify their potential returns by controlling larger positions with a smaller amount of capital. However, as with any tool, its efficacy and safety come from understanding and mastery. For novice traders, the seduction of high leverage can be as enticing as it is perilous. This section aims to demystify leverage, helping you to wield it with confidence and caution in equal measure.

The allure of leverage lies in its ability to magnify gains. When you trade with leverage, you're essentially borrowing funds from your broker to increase your trading position size. Imagine being able to control a $100,000 position in the Forex market with just a $1,000 investment. That's the magic of 100:1 leverage. But, if not handled carefully, the same instrument that amplifies gains can just as easily magnify losses.

It's crucial to approach leverage as you would a double-edged sword. Low capital requirements make leverage an attractive option, but you must remember that with great power comes great responsibility. The potential for amplified losses is a risk you should never overlook. Misunderstanding or misusing leverage can lead to unexpected losses that exceed your initial investment, wiping out your trading account and even putting you in debt.

So, how do you use leverage safely? Start by developing a solid understanding of the concept itself and your own financial limits. Reflect on what amount you can afford to lose without endangering your financial health or peace of mind. Remember, in Forex trading, preservation is just as important as profit. The first rule of using leverage is not to risk more than you are willing and able to lose.

Set sensible leverage ratios that align with your risk tolerance. While some might find 10:1 comfortably manageable, others might prefer to take it down a notch to 5:1. A small leverage ratio doesn't necessarily mean small profits; rather, it signifies a cautious, considered approach that minimizes unnecessary risk. It's about playing the long game, where the focus is on steady growth rather than short-term wins.

The integration of stop-loss orders is another critical component to using leverage safely. By setting predetermined exit points, you can limit losses and secure gains even when you're not actively monitoring the market. This strategy provides an additional layer of protection in volatile markets and shields your account from unexpected price swings.

In addition to stop-loss orders, maintaining a diversified trading portfolio can help mitigate risk. Avoid putting all your eggs in one basket. By spreading risk across various currency pairs and leveraging multiple market opportunities, you reduce the impact of a single trade's potential downturn on your overall portfolio.

Keeping disciplined is easier said than done, especially when the market moves rapidly. Stick to your trading plan and financial goals like a steadfast captain navigating through rough seas. Emotional decision-making often leads to increased risk-taking, particularly when it comes to leveraging positions. Developing a robust mindset that balances rational analysis with intuition can help you sail through challenging times unscathed.

Furthermore, it's important to recognize that even seasoned traders practice caution when using leverage. Continuing education and staying informed about market trends play a significant role in making informed leverage-related decisions. As markets evolve, so should your strategies. The learning never stops, and neither should your awareness of risks associated with leveraged trading.

Finally, back-testing your strategies with demo accounts can be an enlightening experience. This practice allows you to simulate trading scenarios with leverage without risking real capital. Testing different leverage ratios in varied market conditions builds confidence, cultivates patience, and fine-tunes your risk management skills.

In conclusion, leverage is an invaluable asset in Forex trading but only when wielded with caution and precision. It requires an understanding of its mechanics, a commitment to personal financial boundaries, and a strategy that's in tune with market dynamics. By mastering the art of leveraging safely, you're not just amplifying your potential profits; you're also ensuring that you're equipped to handle the market's unpredictability with grace and resilience. This balanced approach enables you to step into the Forex world with not just ambition, but wisdom and readiness to face the challenges ahead.

Chapter 8: Developing a Forex Trading Plan

Stepping into the world of Forex trading without a well-thought-out plan is like sailing without a compass—you're bound to get lost in the turbulent waves of market variations. Crafting a Forex trading plan is crucial as it acts as a roadmap for evaluating trades, managing risks, and achieving your financial goals. A successful plan isn't just about setting strategies; it's about tailoring those strategies to your personal strengths and weaknesses while accounting for market behavior. By establishing clear objectives, defining entry and exit points, and incorporating meticulous risk management tactics, you empower yourself to stay disciplined amidst the market's emotional whirlwind. Remember, consistency is key; a structured plan enhances your ability to make informed decisions rather than impulsive ones, ultimately setting the stage for long-term trading success.

The Importance of a Trading Plan

Embarking on the journey of Forex trading without a well-structured trading plan is like setting sail without a map. In the vast and unpredictable waters of the Forex market, having a clear destination and route is crucial. A trading plan serves as a comprehensive roadmap, guiding new traders through the complexities of the market while helping them maintain focus and discipline. For beginners, a robust trading plan is a foundational pillar for successful trading.

A trading plan outlines your financial goals, strategies, risk tolerance, and much more. Writing it down not only crystallizes your intentions but also serves as a constant reminder of your objectives. By having a written guide, you'll be less swayed by emotions and more grounded in logic. This level of commitment to a plan helps beginners avoid impulsive decisions that often lead to significant losses.

The absence of a plan can be catastrophic. Imagine trying to navigate the bustling currency market without predefined rules and strategies. Traders often fall prey to their biases or emotions, chasing profits without a clear strategy. A trading plan acts as a safeguard against such pitfalls, setting predefined conditions for entering and exiting trades. This can keep you from making decisions based on momentary whims or panic, which are common among those who lack a solid trading foundation.

In addition to setting rules for your trades, a trading plan should reflect your personal trading style and preferences. Are you more comfortable with short-term trades, or do you prefer the potential rewards of long-term positions? These personal choices should be integrated into your plan to create a tailored approach that aligns with your unique strengths and risk appetite.

Risk management is another critical component of any well-devised trading plan. By setting predetermined risk levels for each trade, you protect your capital against unforeseen market movements. Defining how much of your total capital you're willing to risk on a single trade, for instance, provides a clear-cut boundary to maintain your financial health. It also prepares you for potential losses, ensuring that you're trading well within your means.

Moreover, a trading plan enforces discipline. Forex trading can be emotionally taxing, especially during volatile market conditions. Fear and greed are powerful forces that can cloud judgment. A plan acts as an emotional anchor, keeping traders aligned with their initial strategies rather than deviating based on temporary emotions. It helps maintain consistency, which is essential for assessing performance and making informed adjustments over time.

To evaluate your trades effectively, your plan should include specific criteria for measuring success. Establishing clear benchmarks for both winning and losing trades will enable you to analyze your performance objectively. This post-trade analysis is indispensable for continuous improvement. As you track what works and what doesn't, you refine your strategies, increasing your chances of success with each iteration.

Another significant advantage of a detailed trading plan is the ability to stay focused on long-term objectives. Forex trading isn't just about immediate gains but about building wealth over time. A well-considered plan helps you keep your eyes on the prize, minimizing distractions and optimizing your trading process. This focus on the big picture ensures that you remain steadfast and motivated, even during inevitable setbacks.

In the rapidly changing Forex market, flexibility within a trading plan is equally important. While a trading plan provides structure, the ability to adapt to new information or market conditions is crucial. Adjusting your strategies and refining them as you gain experience can help you stay competitive. Your trading plan should be a living document, evolving alongside your growth as a trader.

Finally, creating a trading plan fosters confidence. Uncertainty can be paralyzing, especially for new traders who may feel overwhelmed by the sheer amount of data and potential decisions. A plan demystifies the process, breaking down each trade into manageable steps. This clarity can dramatically improve your confidence level, transforming Forex trading from an intimidating venture into a strategic, manageable activity.

Ultimately, the importance of a trading plan cannot be overstated. It's a critical tool that offers new traders structure, discipline, and clarity amidst the chaos of the Forex market. By committing to a well-crafted trading plan, beginners equip themselves with the necessary tools to navigate and ultimately succeed in the dynamic world of Forex trading.

Components of a Successful Trading Plan

Embarking on a journey into the Forex market without a well-thought-out trading plan is akin to setting sail without a map. Successful traders are not those who rely on luck; instead, they meticulously craft strategies that guide their decisions in a dynamic and often volatile market. Let's delve into the essential components that form a robust trading plan, designed to equip you with the confidence and clarity needed to thrive in Forex trading.

First and foremost, defining your **trading goals** is crucial. These objectives should be as specific, measurable, attainable, relevant, and time-bound as possible. Think about what you want to achieve in the short term and long term. Whether it's generating supplementary income, building a retirement fund, or mastering trading as a full-time career, your goals will shape the rest of your trading plan. Clearly articulating these goals will not only provide direction but also help in measuring your progress.

Understanding your own **risk tolerance** is another cornerstone of any successful trading plan. Every investor has a different threshold for risk, driven by factors such as financial circumstances and personal temperament. A pivotal part of your plan involves assessing how much risk you can realistically take without undue stress or pressure. This self-awareness ensures that you operate within your financial and emotional limits, which can significantly reduce the impact of potential downturns in your trading activities.

The next strategic element is the development of a coherent **trading strategy**. This builds on your goals and risk tolerance to determine how you'll interact with the market. Your strategy will detail how you will enter and exit trades, including the analysis you will employ to make these decisions. Typically, traders use a mixture of technical and fundamental analysis, but the emphasis varies based on personal preference and market conditions. Moreover, this component should also account for how you'll balance and adapt your strategy as new data and trends emerge.

Closely tied to your trading strategy is the implementation of rigorous **risk management techniques**. This involves establishing rules and safeguards to protect your capital. Key components include setting stop-loss orders to prevent excessive loss, defining take-profit levels to secure gains, and deciding the maximum percentage of your portfolio you're willing to risk on any single trade. These measures are not merely protective; they instill discipline, ensuring your actions remain consistent and principled rather than impulsive.

Another essential facet is **record-keeping**. Maintaining comprehensive records of your trades is invaluable for ongoing analysis and growth. Your trading journal should include detailed documentation of trade setups, execution, and outcomes. By continually reviewing your trade history, you can identify patterns, refine strategies, and learn from both your successes and mistakes. This rigorous self-examination transforms experiences into wisdom, progressively sharpening your trading acumen.

Market analysis forms a vital component of your trading plan. Regularly analyzing the market keeps you attuned to shifts that could affect your trading. A combination of fundamental analysis—for example, watching economic indicators—and technical analysis, such as observing chart patterns and indicators, is crucial for making informed decisions. Your plan should clearly define how you'll conduct these analyses, the tools you'll use, and how often you'll review market conditions to keep your approach dynamic and informed.

In parallel, don't overlook the significance of maintaining the right **trader mindset**. Trading, at times, can be emotionally taxing. Cultivating patience, discipline, and emotional resilience is part of the journey. Establishing routines and practices that foster mental fortitude can significantly enhance your decision-making prowess. Consider techniques like mindfulness or visualization to help manage stress and maintain focus during challenging market phases.

Your trading plan should also address **technology and resources**. Identify the tools and platforms that will facilitate your trading activities. This includes choosing the right trading platform, securing reliable data feeds, and employing analysis software that suits your needs. Furthermore, continually expanding your knowledge base through education and networking with other traders enriches your approach. A well-rounded strategy incorporates a commitment to ongoing learning, ensuring you stay ahead of market innovations and trends.

Finally, embrace **flexibility** and adaptability. While having a structured plan is essential, markets are inherently unpredictable. Your ability to adjust and refine your approach based on practical experiences and emerging market realities is crucial for sustained success. Regularly revisiting and updating your trading plan ensures that it remains relevant and aligned with your evolving goals and market conditions.

In conclusion, constructing a successful trading plan is a multifaceted process that demands introspection, discipline, and continuous refinement. Each component, from goal setting and risk management to market analysis and psychological resilience, plays a critical role in shaping a trader capable of navigating the Forex market's complexities. Equip yourself with this robust framework to not only survive but thrive in this ever-changing financial landscape.

Chapter 9: Using Forex Trading Platforms

In the dynamic realm of Forex trading, selecting and mastering a trading platform is pivotal for a budding trader's success. Platforms function as your digital gateway to the market, offering an array of tools that enhance your trading journey. Navigating these platforms efficiently can make or break your trading experience, so they are designed to be user-friendly to ensure seamless execution of trades. To gain confidence, beginning with a demo account is incredibly beneficial; it allows you to practice strategies and familiarize yourself with the platform without risking real money. As you progress, your mastery of placing trades and responding to market movements becomes intuitive, empowering you to act decisively. Engaging with these platforms equips you with real-time data, analytical tools, and charting features that are essential for making informed decisions. Embrace the learning curve, for in honing these skills, you lay the foundation for a prosperous trading future.

Navigating Trading Software

Diving into the world of Forex trading for the first time might seem overwhelming, especially with the array of trading software available to you. But mastering your trading platform is your ticket to unlocking the Forex market's potential. Think of your trading software as the control center for all your Forex activities. It's where you analyze market data, execute trades, and manage your portfolio. Let's break down how to effectively navigate these platforms so that you can trade with confidence.

Most Forex trading platforms are comprehensive tools filled with functionalities designed to assist you in making informed decisions. The interface typically includes price charts, market orders, account balance details, and a host of other tools. Familiarizing yourself with these components is crucial as they form the backbone of your decision-making process. Location of elements might vary, but understanding what each tool offers can simplify your trading decisions enormously.

One of the most crucial aspects of any trading platform is the price chart. Price charts are visual representations of market data that help traders like you track currency pairs' price movements. Whether you prefer candlestick, line, or bar charts, learning how to read and interpret these is key. Charts can display different time frames—from one minute to weekly views—which allows you to see short-term trends or long-term patterns. Analyzing these visuals aids in forecasting potential market moves, making it an indispensable part of your trading toolkit.

While charts visualize data, the analytical powerhouses are the built-in indicators and tools. Technical indicators such as moving averages, Bollinger bands, or MACD (Moving Average Convergence Divergence) provide insights into market trends and potential turnarounds. These tools can be intimidating at first, with mathematics and jargon to understand, but they soon become second nature with practice. Using these indicators wisely can improve your trading accuracy, helping you make informed and precise decisions.

Your trading software will also feature an order panel, an equally vital component. Here, you'll execute trades, set stop-loss orders, and manage your account position. It is crucial to understand the different order types, such as market orders, limit orders, and stop orders. Each order type serves a specific purpose. For instance, market orders let you buy or sell at the best available price immediately, while limit orders execute trades at a specific or better price. Grasping these elements allows you to execute trades efficiently, reducing costly mistakes.

Another essential feature to become acquainted with is the platform's toolbox for risk management. Risk management is a discipline unto itself in Forex trading, and well-configured trading software can help you practice it efficiently. The software allows for setting predetermined stop-loss or take-profit points, ensuring your trades automatically close once certain market conditions are met. Having this safety net can save you from emotional decision-making, giving you peace of mind that your losses are capped.

Platforms often come loaded with news feeds and economic calendars—tools that traders rely on to practice fundamental analysis. These features keep you informed about market-shaking events, like economic announcements and geopolitical developments. By feeding you real-time news, the trading platform acts like a hub for current information, keeping you a step ahead of the game. Coupling this with your analysis tools enhances your ability to respond to the market with agility and insight.

Most trading platforms offer customization options that let you tailor the interface to suit your trading style. Customizing charts, setting up a preferred indicator layout, and choosing notifications that work for you can transform your trading experience from robotic to fluid. By personalizing your workspace, you create an environment where you can function best—staying focused and efficient.

Transitioning to actual trading practice, platforms often incorporate features that support simulated trading or demo accounts. These accounts are priceless as they allow you to navigate through trades with play money but in real market conditions. They're excellent for getting acquainted with the platform's mechanics without the risk of losing money. Through practice, you'll gain confidence and insight into what real trading will feel like, all while honing your strategies.

If difficulties arise, most platforms are backed with community forums and customer support that can help troubleshoot any issues. These resources can be a treasure trove of information as other traders share tips and experiences. Engaging with such platforms can deepen your understanding and may also introduce you to new trading techniques or strategies you can try in your safe demo environment.

Lastly, maintaining peace of mind through dependable platforms cannot be overemphasized. Choosing a reliable platform known for its security features ensures that your data remains protected. Make sure your chosen software uses encryption and adheres to regulatory standards. A secure trading environment allows you to concentrate on analyzing and trading rather than worrying about the safety of your personal and financial information.

In summary, a well-mastered trading platform is a gateway to successful forex trading. Familiarizing yourself with its features, effective risk management elements, and practice tools creates a sturdy foundation. Whether it's through understanding charts, using indicators, or customizing your setup, mastering these aspects equips you to become an informed, confident trader. Remember, the right software doesn't just facilitate trades—it enhances your trading journey, helping you make the most of market opportunities.

Demo Accounts and Their Benefits

As you step into the world of Forex trading, one of the most invaluable tools at your disposal is a *demo account*. Think of it as your training ground, where you can experiment without fear of loss. A demo account offers a risk-free environment to learn the ropes of Forex trading using virtual money. These accounts simulate real market conditions, providing an essential bridge between theory and practice. Whether you're trying out new strategies or familiarizing yourself with the trading platform's features, a demo account is where it all begins.

The benefits of using a demo account are manifold. For one, you get to learn the mechanics of trading platforms. As each platform may differ slightly, demo accounts allow you to understand navigation, order execution, and other technical functionalities without the stress of real stakes. Being well-versed in these operations ensures that when you're ready to transition to actual trading, you can focus on strategy rather than fumbling with the platform.

Furthermore, demo accounts offer a stress-free way to develop and test your trading strategy. They provide a playground for trial and error. Here, there's no real money involved, so you can take risks and learn from mistakes without financial consequences. This experimentation is crucial to refine your approach, understand what works, and identify potential pitfalls in your strategy. By spending ample time honing your plan within a demo account, you're setting yourself up for increased confidence when venturing into live trading.

Another advantage is the opportunity to get a feel for market dynamics. While demo accounts use simulated money, the data feed and price movements mirror real market conditions. This parallel allows you to observe how currency pairs react to various economic events and news releases. Understanding these market fluctuations is imperative for developing the timing and urgency needed in live situations.

Moreover, demo accounts aid in the development of emotional resilience. Fear and greed are powerful emotions in trading, often leading to impulsive decisions. Using a demo account allows you to experience emotional ups and downs in a controlled setting. Over time, you learn to manage these emotions, improving your emotional discipline. This emotional training is equally as important as understanding the technical aspects of trading.

Many traders also use demo accounts for benchmarking performance. They track success rates, document outcomes of different strategies, and study their own trading behaviors. This analytical approach helps in identifying strengths and weaknesses. By regularly reflecting on these findings, you can set realistic goals and maintain a gradual progression toward being a proficient trader.

Additionally, demo accounts are a crucial tool for familiarizing yourself with leverage and margin without real financial exposure. Understanding these concepts in a simulated environment enables better risk management once you move on to a live account. You can explore different leverage settings and see firsthand how they affect your trades, gaining a deeper understanding of risks and rewards.

Finally, demo accounts offer the convenience of practice without time constraints. There's no pressure to go live before you're ready. You can practice at your own pace until you feel confident enough to transition. This flexibility fosters a learning environment tailored to your personal schedule and progress rate.

In sum, demo accounts provide a comprehensive platform to prepare for live Forex trading. They instill confidence, build technical skills, and develop emotional stability. So, embrace this valuable tool, and use it to its full potential. Once you're ready to advance to a live account, you'll appreciate the solid foundation you've built.

Placing Trades in a Trading Platform

When stepping into the Forex trading arena, one of the most crucial skills you'll need is how to place trades on a trading platform. Understanding this process is vital because it's your primary tool for executing trade decisions. It's the bridge between your strategy and the market, and mastering it can empower you to seize opportunities as they arise. Let's dive into how you can confidently place trades within a Forex trading platform, keeping in mind the profound impact this can have on your trading journey.

Firstly, every trade begins with selecting the currency pair you wish to trade. Most platforms have a comprehensive list of available pairs, ranging from the major ones like EUR/USD to more exotic options. Knowing which pair to trade stems from your analysis and strategy, but the platform gives you the stage to enact your choice. Look for the search feature in your trading platform to quickly locate the pair you want to explore. Once you've found it, a simple click usually displays detailed information like current prices and spread costs. This functionality is straightforward but crucial to launching the trading process correctly.

With the currency pair selected, it's time to decide whether you're going long or short—terms we discussed earlier in this book. In a nutshell, going long means you are buying the first currency in the pair, betting that its value will rise against the second. If you're going short, you're selling the first currency, speculating that its value will decline. Most platforms will present these options clearly, often with prominent buy and sell buttons, making it easy for you to execute your intended strategy.

Once you've decided on your position, the next step involves specifying trade details like the size of your trade, often measured in lots. Deciding on the trade size requires balancing the potential for profit with the risk of loss, a skill sharpened by experience and understanding the leverage and margin concepts explained earlier. Most platforms offer intuitive ways to adjust the trade size, often via dropdowns or direct input fields.

Moreover, you should set up stop-loss and take-profit orders. These tools are essential for effective risk management, allowing you to control the losses or lock in profits when prices hit certain levels. A stop-loss order automatically closes a trade that moves against you beyond a pre-set limit, preventing further losses. Conversely, a take-profit order locks in profits once the trade reaches a favorable price level. Properly using these tools helps mitigate emotional trading decisions, keeping your strategy on track.

Execution speed is another aspect every aspiring trader should consider. Most modern trading platforms offer real-time data and fast execution speeds, meaning that your orders are processed almost instantaneously. However, market conditions can occasionally delay executions, so it's important to stay informed and be prepared for instances where you might not get the exact price you expect. This highlights the importance of staying updated with platform news and understanding how different types of orders, like market orders versus limit orders, can impact your trading.

Market orders execute immediately at the current price, while limit orders execute at a price you specify. Choosing the right order type is an essential part of strategic planning. If speed is critical, a market order might be your best option. But if you're after precision and are willing to wait, a limit order can be more advantageous. Each has its place in a well-rounded trading strategy and underscores the flexibility good traders develop over time.

Temperature checks, or reviewing your trade set-up before final execution, are highly advisable. It's easy to overlook details in the hustle of the trading process. Take a moment to double-check everything—currency pair, trade size, order type, stop-loss, and take-profit settings—to ensure they align with your strategy. Once everything is verified, you've reached the moment of truth: executing the trade. Confirm the trade and monitor your account to see how it evolves.

Trading platforms typically provide complex analytics and reporting tools. As your trade progresses, utilize these features to gain insights. Live feed charts, profitability summaries, and trading history logs can help you understand current performance and guide future decisions. Reviewing your trades, both good and bad, fosters continuous learning. It's about seeing which strategies resonate well and which require recalibration, helping you to grow into a more proficient trader.

Lastly, technology is continually advancing in trading platforms, with innovations like algorithmic trading and automation tools making their mark. These features can be game-changers, allowing traders to set parameters for trades to execute automatically based on predefined criteria. They offer an additional layer of precision and remove some of the emotion from trading. Even if you're starting with manual trades, being aware of these features is critical, as they could become instrumental as you refine your approach.

In conclusion, placing trades on a Forex trading platform is an intricate process requiring both understanding and practice. By efficiently navigating currency pair selection, order types, and risk management tools, you gain the confidence to execute trades that align with your strategic vision. With experience, this process will become second nature, paving the way to informed and calculated trades. Remember, every trade is a step toward mastering the Forex market and achieving trading success.

Chapter 10: Understanding Forex Brokers

Forex brokers play a crucial role in your trading journey, serving as intermediaries between traders and the currency markets. Before diving into trading, it's essential to understand how brokers operate and how they impact your success. Different types of brokers, such as market makers and electronic communication networks (ECNs), offer various services and fee structures, potentially affecting your trading costs and execution speed. Selecting the right broker for you can be daunting, yet it's one of the most decisive steps for securing a reliable trading experience. Start by evaluating brokers based on their reputation, regulatory compliance, trading platforms, and customer support. A good broker should offer transparency in their operations and provide educational resources to help you grow as a trader. By choosing a broker that aligns with your trading style and needs, you empower yourself to navigate the complexities of the Forex market with greater confidence.

How Brokers Operate

Understanding how brokers operate is crucial for anyone venturing into the world of Forex trading. These financial intermediaries play a vital role in facilitating trade execution, providing the conduit through which traders can enter the vast currency market. Brokers offer platforms and tools essential for buying and selling currency pairs, and their functioning can significantly impact your trading experience.

At the core, Forex brokers act as the middlemen between the traders and the interbank exchange market. The interbank market comprises a network of banks exchanging currencies between themselves, but for individual traders or smaller entities, accessing this market directly isn't feasible. Brokers step in to bridge this gap, allowing individuals to execute trades through their networks.

One essential aspect of broker operation is the execution model they employ. This can greatly affect the spread, speed, and overall cost of your trades. Broadly, there are two main models: Market Maker and Electronic Communication Network (ECN). Market Makers create their market for clients and typically offer fixed spreads. On the other hand, ECNs aggregate prices from different liquidity providers, often offering tighter spreads but with variable rates depending on market conditions. Both models have their advantages, and understanding them can help you decide which aligns better with your trading strategy.

When we delve deeper, transparency and trust become crucial concerns. A broker's reputation hinges on their regulatory compliance and the transparency of their operations. Regulatory bodies like the Financial Conduct Authority (FCA), Commodity Futures Trading Commission (CFTC), and others across the globe ensure that brokers maintain a standard of operation, protecting trader funds and enforcing fair trade practices. It's vital to interact with brokers who are under stringent regulation, providing an extra layer of confidence and security.

Additionally, brokers offer leverage, which amplifies a trader's buying power. This service, while beneficial in increasing potential returns, comes with heightened risk. Brokers require traders to meet certain margin requirements, a safety net to ensure there's enough coverage for potential losses. Understanding how brokers calculate and enforce these requirements helps traders manage their risk more effectively. The broker, therefore, plays a pivotal role not just in executing trades but also in establishing the parameters within which trades occur.

Beyond facilitating trades, many brokers provide educational resources to help traders learn and refine their strategies. These resources range from articles and video tutorials to webinars and interactive courses. For newcomers, this can be an invaluable addition, helping them grasp the fundamentals and move towards more advanced trading concepts. The level of customer service and educational support a broker offers can make a huge difference in a trader's learning curve and confidence.

Technology also features prominently in how brokers operate. The shift towards digital has meant that a broker's choice of platform can be a make-or-break factor for traders. User-friendly interfaces, real-time data feeds, and fast execution speeds can enhance trading efficiency. Moreover, many brokers offer mobile applications, allowing traders to manage their accounts on the go, which adds to the flexibility and convenience of Forex trading today.

The fee structures of brokers also differ and can include spreads, commissions, or a combination of both. Some brokers might advertise zero commissions but might have higher spreads, while others charge a small fee per trade with tighter spreads. This can greatly impact your trading costs over time, especially for frequent traders. Therefore, understanding the cost implications of different brokers is vital for managing your trading expenses effectively.

Lastly, the importance of demo accounts cannot be overstated. Brokers who offer demo accounts provide an invaluable opportunity for traders to familiarize themselves with the trading platform, test strategies, and gain practical experience without financial risk. This feature allows traders to experiment and hone their skills, making transitions to live trading smoother and more informed.

In conclusion, how brokers operate is multifaceted and impacts all areas of the trading process. From execution models, regulatory compliance, leverage provision, to technology and fees, each element has its place in ensuring effective trade facilitation. Understanding these nuances equips traders to make more informed broker choices, aligning them with partners who best match their trading preferences and objectives.

Types of Forex Brokers

When you're diving into the world of Forex trading, understanding the different types of brokers is essential for your journey. Forex brokers are the intermediaries between you and the foreign exchange market, and they come in various forms. The broker type can significantly influence factors such as trading costs, execution speed, and your overall trading experience. It's important to recognize these types to ensure you're choosing one that aligns with your trading strategy and goals.

Broadly speaking, the two primary classifications of Forex brokers are **Dealing Desk (DD) brokers** and **No Dealing Desk (NDD) brokers**. Let's explore what sets them apart.

Dealing Desk brokers, also known as market makers, operate on a model where they take the opposite side of the trade. They provide liquidity to the market by creating a market for you. Essentially, when you buy a currency pair, a Dealing Desk broker sells it to you and vice versa. This mechanism allows them to set their own bid and ask prices, which might include a spread or mark-up. Some traders view this with suspicion, fearing potential conflicts of interest. However, for many retail traders, market makers offer a simple and straightforward entry into the Forex world, often providing fixed spreads and robust trading platforms.

In contrast, *No Dealing Desk brokers* connect traders directly to the interbank market, providing access to real market prices without interference. This category can be further divided into **Electronic Communication Network (ECN)** brokers and **Straight Through Processing (STP)** brokers. ECN brokers are facilitators, enabling client orders to interact with other participants in the network, ensuring tighter spreads and more transparency. Orders are matched directly to the best available bid/ask prices from market participants, including banks and other traders. However, this transparency often comes with additional costs, such as commissions on trades.

On the other hand, STP brokers, while similar to ECNs, usually send orders directly to liquidity providers, often using several different providers for better pricing. This typically ensures faster execution and reduced re-quotes. Unlike ECN brokers, STP brokers might not have a visible depth of market, but they still offer competitive spreads, which can be floating or variable, depending on the market volatility.

For newcomers, choosing between these types can feel overwhelming. It involves weighing factors like costs, speed of execution, and potential conflicts of interest. Market conditions and personal preferences often dictate the choice. If you're looking for more transparency and potentially lower spreads, in exchange for paying a commission, an ECN might suit you best. Alternatively, if you'd rather have a simpler trading experience with straightforward costs, a Market Maker could be the way to go.

An important consideration when choosing a Forex broker is their regulatory status. Regulatory bodies, such as the U.S. Commodity Futures Trading Commission (CFTC), the Financial Conduct Authority (FCA) in the UK, and the Australian Securities and Investments Commission (ASIC), impose strict compliance standards to protect traders. A regulated broker provides a level of security and reassurance that your funds are protected, and trading activities are monitored under a framework of rules designed to ensure fair treatment.

Additionally, many brokers are now offering instant execution services, appealing to traders who look for certainty in the execution prices of their trades. This is sometimes contrasted with market execution, where trades are executed at the best available price in the market, which could differ slightly from the requested price in times of high volatility. Understanding these execution models will help in assessing the potential slippage during order fulfillment.

Some brokers offer both types of brokerages, labeled as **hybrid brokers**. These brokers might operate as market makers for smaller trades or less popular currency pairs, while utilizing ECN or STP executions for higher-volume or more popular trades. This combination allows brokers to cater to a broader range of traders' needs and preferences.

Another key distinction is the presence of a service called **Direct Market Access (DMA)**. DMA offers a complete range of assets with more precise pricing directly from the source, usually at the expense of flexible trading conditions. For professional traders who appreciate delving deeper into market intricacies, DMA provides valuable insights and substantial trading advantages.

When considering the type of broker to choose, it's crucial to reflect on what kind of trading you'll be doing. For instance, day traders and scalpers require tight spreads and quick execution, often opting for ECN brokers. In contrast, swing traders or those trading over longer periods might not prioritize spreads as heavily and are content with the offerings of a market maker.

Moreover, any broker you choose should offer a robust trading platform, providing you with essential tools and functionalities necessary for analyzing the market and executing trades. Access to complimentary educational resources, real-time news feeds, and customer support services are invaluable added services that typically enhance the trader's experience.

Ultimately, understanding the types of Forex brokers arms you with the knowledge to make informed decisions, equipping you with the confidence to navigate the forex market. Proper due diligence ensures the selected broker aligns with your trading objectives and that you're adequately supported on your Forex trading journey.

As you progress in your trading career, the flexibility to adapt and possibly switch between broker types depending on evolving strategies and market conditions will become an invaluable skill. Remember, your broker is your partner in the Forex market, and the right broker can offer immense support in achieving your trading aspirations.

Choosing the Right Broker for You

Embarking on your forex trading journey requires more than just understanding the basics of currency pairs or leverage. An essential step in your trading success is choosing the right broker—one that aligns with your goals and trading style. With numerous brokers vying for your attention, it's crucial to make a well-informed decision. This section aims to guide you through the key factors to consider when selecting a broker, ensuring you start on the right foot.

First, think about the broker's regulatory status. A regulated broker offers a layer of security, safeguarding your funds and maintaining fair trading practices. Regulatory bodies such as the Commodity Futures Trading Commission (CFTC) in the U.S. or the Financial Conduct Authority (FCA) in the UK impose strict requirements on brokers, enhancing transparency and accountability. Choose brokers regulated by reputable authorities to ensure your investments are protected.

Consider the trading conditions a broker offers as well. This includes spreads, commissions, and leverage ratios. A lower spread can significantly impact your profitability, particularly if you're engaging in high-frequency trading. Some brokers offer fixed spreads, while others offer variable ones, so understanding the difference can influence which broker is best suited for you. Additionally, be clear about commission structures, as this could affect your bottom line.

Leverage options are another essential consideration. While leverage can amplify your profits, it also increases your risk. Different brokers offer varying leverage ratios, often depending on their regulatory environment. Ensure the leverage options align with your risk tolerance and trading strategy. It's wise to start with lower leverage if you're new to trading to manage risk better.

The types of accounts offered can also influence your decision. Brokers typically offer several account types, including standard, mini, and micro accounts. A standard account might require a higher minimum deposit but offers full trading capabilities. Mini or micro accounts allow you to start trading with less capital, which is beneficial for beginners testing their strategies.

Then there's the trading platform. A reliable and user-friendly trading platform can markedly improve your trading experience. The platform should offer real-time data, advanced charting tools, and effective order execution. Additionally, consider whether the platform is web-based or requires downloads, and if it offers mobile trading options. The ease of accessing your trades on-the-go can be a game-changer for many traders.

Customer support is an often-overlooked factor but can make a big difference when dealing with technical glitches or account issues. Opt for brokers that offer 24/7 customer service with multiple contact channels such as phone, email, and live chat. An efficient and responsive support team is invaluable in resolving issues quickly, minimizing downtime.

The number and variety of financial instruments available for trading should also align with your trading objectives. While some traders focus solely on forex pairs, others diversify into commodities or indices. Check if the broker supports the instruments you wish to trade, as it can affect your strategy development and execution.

Another aspect to evaluate is the broker's reputation and user reviews. While no broker is without criticism, a consistent pattern of complaints might be a red flag. Engage with trading communities and forums to gather genuine feedback about brokers' reliability and trustworthiness. Personal experiences can provide insights that go beyond what's displayed on a broker's website.

Furthermore, pay attention to educational resources and research tools offered by the broker. Rich educational materials can enhance your trading skills—especially important if you're new to forex trading. Some brokers provide webinars, tutorials, and market analysis reports that help you stay informed and confident in your trading decisions.

Deposit and withdrawal processes also matter. The ease of depositing funds into your account and the speed at which you can withdraw them play a role in your overall satisfaction. Investigate any hidden fees or processing times to ensure there are no surprises later on. Transparent processes are indicative of a broker that values client relationships.

Lastly, trial the broker through a demo account. Before committing your hard-earned money, a demo account lets you test the platform's functionality and trading conditions without risk. It's a safe space to refine your strategies and understand the nuances of the trading platform in a risk-free environment. Most reputable brokers offer this option, making it an indispensable step before going live.

Choosing the right broker is not a decision to rush. It's a foundational element that can significantly influence your trading journey. Take your time, do your research, and select a broker that aligns with your financial goals and trading style. With the right broker by your side, you'll be well-equipped to navigate the dynamic world of forex trading with confidence and competence.

Chapter 11:
The Psychology of Forex Trading

Diving into the psychology of Forex trading is like harnessing the key to mastering your inner game. Successful trading involves more than just technical analysis or strategy; it demands emotional discipline and self-awareness. Every decision you make has a psychological component, whether it's the elation of a victory or the sting of a loss. This chapter focuses on understanding how emotions can often cloud judgment and lead to impulsive decisions, emphasizing the need to stay cool-headed and objective. Developing a trader's mindset isn't just about controlling emotions but also building resilience in the face of inevitable ups and downs. Remember, the best traders are those who don't let wins go to their head or losses to their heart. Cultivating these traits can transform you into a trader who doesn't just react to the market but interacts with it strategically and calmly.

Emotional Discipline and Trading

Emotional discipline in trading is a cornerstone skill that every aspiring forex trader needs to master. Trading is not solely about analyzing charts and making predictions based on economic indicators; it's equally about controlling the emotions that can impact your decision-making process. In the dynamic and often unpredictable forex market, emotions like fear, greed, and hope play a significant role in influencing traders' actions. Understanding how to manage these emotions can mean the difference between consistent profit and substantial loss.

To begin with, fear is a powerful emotion that can trigger a chain reaction of detrimental decisions. Often, fear manifests when trades do not go as planned, leading traders to panic and make impulsive decisions. For instance, a trader might be inclined to prematurely exit a position at a loss, only to see the market reverse shortly after. This impetuous reaction, driven by fear of further loss, often overrides logical and strategic thinking. Learning to recognize when fear is dictating your actions is the first step in maintaining emotional discipline.

On the other hand, greed can be equally problematic. The excitement of winning trades and the lure of potential profits can drive traders to overtrade or engage in riskier trades than their strategy allows. Greed can cloud judgment, leading one to hold onto winning trades for too long with the hope of maximizing profits, only to watch them revert into losses. Developing discipline means setting clear profit targets and sticking to them, irrespective of the temptation to chase more gains.

Hope, although often seen as a positive emotion, can also be a hindrance in trading. Holding onto losing positions in the hope that the market will turn around can lead to deeper losses. It is essential for traders to detach their emotions from trading decisions and adhere strictly to predetermined plans and stop-loss orders. Solid strategies are based on research and analysis, not hope.

The path to emotional discipline in trading demands practice and self-awareness. It's crucial to develop a strong mindset oriented toward long-term success rather than short-lived victories. Successful traders cultivate patience and resilience. They understand that losses are part of the game and are often necessary lessons in fine-tuning strategies.

This perspective helps in maintaining composure and focus amid market volatility.

Creating a detailed trading plan is one of the most effective strategies for maintaining emotional discipline. A trading plan outlines specific entry and exit criteria, risk management rules, and strategies tailored to financial goals. It serves as a roadmap, guiding traders and keeping emotions in check as they face market fluctuations. Following the plan rigidly, even when emotions run high, separates disciplined traders from those swayed by temporary market conditions.

Furthermore, journaling trades is a useful practice for developing emotional discipline. Keeping a detailed record of each trade, along with the emotions felt during the trade, can provide invaluable insight into recurring emotional patterns that impact performance. Reviewing these notes regularly allows traders to identify areas for improvement and recognize emotion-driven mistakes. Over time, this reflective process strengthens emotional regulation skills.

Meditation and mindfulness techniques can also be significant allies for traders striving for emotional discipline. These practices enhance focus and concentration, reduce stress, and cultivate a calm and balanced emotional state. Incorporating daily mindfulness exercises can help traders develop the mental clarity needed to execute trades without emotional interference effectively.

An integral component of emotional discipline is the ability to take a step back and assess the situation objectively. Practicing self-compassion and acknowledging that mistakes and losses are learning opportunities rather than failures can shift one's mindset. This shift encourages improved trading practices, boosts confidence, and mitigates the emotional turmoil that often overwhelms beginners.

Lastly, connecting with a community of traders can provide substantial emotional support. Engaging with others who understand the challenges and pressures of forex trading can alleviate feelings of isolation and help manage stress. Whether through online forums or local meetups, exchanging experiences and insights fosters resilience and strengthens the emotional fortitude required for successful trading.

In conclusion, emotional discipline is not something traders achieve overnight. It's a continuous journey of self-improvement and learning. By acknowledging the impact of emotions and developing strategies to manage them, traders stand a much higher chance of achieving consistent success. Embracing emotional discipline in trading isn't just about improving market outcomes; it's about cultivating a mindset that serves well beyond the trading floor.

Overcoming Psychological Challenges

Trading in the Forex market is not just a game of numbers and charts; it's a deeply psychological endeavor that challenges traders in unique ways. Perhaps one of the most daunting barriers for newcomers is the array of psychological challenges they face. Whether it's fear of loss or the constant pressure to succeed, these mental barriers can impede even the most knowledgeable traders if not properly addressed. So, how do we begin to overcome these hurdles?

First, it's crucial to understand the role emotions play in trading. Fear and greed are often cited as the two most detrimental emotional states for traders. Fear can prevent you from executing trades when opportunities are ripe, while greed might push you to take unnecessary risks. Balancing these emotions requires emotional discipline and self-awareness. By integrating mindfulness and self-reflection into your routine, you create mental space to assess your emotional state before making trading decisions.

Mindfulness, however, is not an easy skill to master. It demands practice and consistency. Start by taking a moment to pause and reflect before executing any trade. Ask yourself if your decision is based on a sound trading strategy or if it's influenced by the fear of missing out or the desire to recover losses quickly. This simple practice can dramatically reduce impulsive trading decisions and help maintain a rational perspective. Remember, it's better to miss a trade than to enter a bad one.

Managing stress is another critical aspect of overcoming psychological challenges in Forex trading. The markets can be unpredictable and unforgiving, which naturally leads to stress, especially when live trading involves real money. The key to handling stress is developing a structured trading plan that helps mitigate unpredictable elements. Having a clear set of guidelines and strategies can provide a sense of control and reduce anxiety.

Incorporate healthy habits outside of trading to help manage stress levels. Regular exercise, a balanced diet, and adequate sleep contribute to overall mental well-being. Don't underestimate the power of taking breaks. A fresh mind is far more effective than a clouded, weary one. Step away from your screen, especially after intense sessions, to give your mind the rest it needs.

Yet, perhaps the most profound psychological challenge is the blow to one's confidence following a significant loss. Every trader experiences losses; accepting them as a part of the journey is crucial. What's more important is how you respond to those losses. Instead of viewing them as failures, see them as learning opportunities. Each loss offers insights into potential mistakes and areas for improvement. Review your trading journal (yes, keeping one is highly recommended) to dissect what went wrong and how similar errors can be avoided in the future.

Building resilience in trading is akin to building muscle. It requires practice, repetition, and sometimes stepping out of one's comfort zone. Engage with communities or seek mentorship from seasoned traders who can provide not only advice but also emotional support. Talking to others who've faced similar challenges can be profoundly reassuring and inspiring.

Here's another psychological hurdle: the relentless pursuit of perfection. New traders often fall into the trap of believing that every trade must be a success. This mindset leads to unnecessary pressure and unrealistically high expectations. The truth is, no trader, no matter how experienced, wins all the time. Accepting imperfections and understanding that the goal is to achieve consistent profitability over time, rather than winning every trade, can reduce this pressure.

Visualization and positive affirmations can also be beneficial. These techniques, often used by athletes, can help cultivate a positive outlook. Before starting your trading day, visualize yourself calmly executing your strategy. Affirmations like "I am a disciplined trader" or "I manage risk effectively" can reinforce your confidence and composure.

Ultimately, overcoming psychological challenges in Forex trading is about cultivating a balanced mindset that combines analytical thinking with emotional intelligence. It requires continuous self-assessment and a commitment to personal and professional growth. Remember, whether you're trading with virtual or real money, your mental capital is one of your most valuable assets.

As you gain more experience, these psychological hurdles may become less daunting. However, always remain vigilant. The market is an ever-evolving beast, and maintaining your mental edge is as crucial as understanding any trading indicator or strategy.

In conclusion, Forex trading is as much about psychology as it is about strategy. Overcoming psychological challenges is a continuous journey of self-improvement, discipline, and emotional growth. By recognizing and addressing these challenges head-on, you'll position yourself not just as a better trader, but as a more resilient one, ready to navigate the complexities of the Forex landscape confidently.

Developing a Trader's Mindset

Delving into the world of Forex trading can feel like stepping onto a new planet. You're learning a unique language, deciphering charts, and navigating complex tools. But beneath all this technicality lies a critical component: the trader's mindset. Without this, even the most meticulously planned strategies can falter. A successful trader isn't just someone proficient with numbers and data; they're someone who understands and masters their emotions and mindset.

First, let's consider why mindset matters so much in trading. Forex trading isn't just about currencies and analysis; it encompasses human behavior, emotions, and psychology. Human beings aren't robots, and the decisions made on the trading floor are influenced by emotions such as fear and greed. Ever felt the rush of excitement after a successful trade or the sharp sting of regret after a loss? You're not alone. These emotions are natural, but how you manage them can distinguish you from less successful traders.

Instilling emotional discipline is one of the first steps in developing a trader's mindset. Emotional discipline means remaining calm and collected irrespective of the market's ups or downs. It's about sticking to your trading plan and not letting the fear of missing out (FOMO) push you into rash decisions. You must remember that every experienced trader has faced setbacks; the difference lies in how they handle these setbacks and move forward.

To anchor yourselves against emotional tides, consider practicing mindfulness. This involves being fully present and aware of your emotions without letting them control your actions. Regularly check in with yourself before you enter or exit a trade. Are you acting out of excitement, fear, or overconfidence? Awareness is key to reigning in impulsive actions that might lead to significant losses.

Next comes cultivating patience, a virtue most traders find challenging. The Forex market isn't a place for instant gratification. It isn't a slot machine where you pull a lever and wait for payouts. Opportunities often emerge slowly, and sometimes the best action is inaction. Learning to wait for the right moments can save you from unnecessary risks and help maximize returns over time. In this context, patience isn't passivity; it's a strategic pause to seize the right opportunity.

Confidence also plays a pivotal role, but it needs to be balanced. Overconfidence can be detrimental; it may push you to risk more than your trading plan allows, based on the assumption that you can't be wrong. On the flip side, lack of confidence can paralyze decision-making, leading you to miss valuable opportunities. The sweet spot is in having confidence backed by solid strategies and knowledge.

Developing resilience is essential in molding a sturdy trader's mindset. Trading involves facing losses, and these aren't just financial setbacks; they test your psychological grit. How you handle these losses will determine your longevity in the market. Reflect on your trades, learn from mistakes, and adapt your strategies accordingly. Viewing losses as learning experiences rather than personal failures helps build resilience and strengthen your trading prowess.

Having a growth mindset is another vital aspect. Trading is dynamic; markets evolve, and so do strategies. A fixed mindset might hinder your progress by keeping you rigid against changes and new information. Instead, be open to continuous learning. Every day in the market is an opportunity to expand your knowledge, refine your techniques, and improve your results. Remember, the goal isn't perfection but consistent improvement and adaptability.

Setting realistic goals will also fortify your mindset. Entering the Forex market with unattainable expectations is a recipe for disappointment. Instead, create achievable milestones, celebrate small victories, and gradually build your way up. Realistic goals ground your trading efforts in practicality, helping you maintain motivation even during challenging periods.

It's crucial not to isolate yourself in this journey. Networking with other traders can offer support and shared experiences. Engaging with a community of like-minded individuals provides insights into different strategies and perspectives. While personal trading skills are invaluable, learning from the successes and failures of others can accelerate your growth.

Feedback plays a crucial role in refining your mindset and skillset. Regularly review your trading journal—it should document trades executed, the reasoning behind decisions, and emotional responses during those times. Identifying patterns in these entries can help in understanding emotional triggers and adjusting your approach accordingly.

Remember, no one becomes a master trader overnight. Tactical skills need to be honed, and the psychological component demands equal attention and effort. Developing a trader's mindset is a continuous process where knowledge, emotional fortitude, and strategic thinking converge.

In summary, embracing the journey to develop a trader's mindset is as essential as understanding technical analysis or market trends. It empowers you to navigate the volatile Forex landscape with confidence, patience, and resilience. By focusing on emotional discipline, resilience, and a growth mindset, you'll be better equipped to harness the potential of your trading endeavors. Approach each trade, not just as a transaction but as an opportunity for growth and learning. With time, you'll find yourself making informed decisions that lead to sustained success in this dynamic market.

Chapter 12: Staying Informed and Evolving

Stepping into the Forex arena is just the beginning of your financial journey. Embracing the spirit of lifelong learning and adaptation is crucial to navigating the ever-evolving Forex market landscape. Staying informed doesn't simply mean keeping up with the latest headlines; it requires cultivating a keen sense of curiosity and an open mind to new strategies and insights. Engage with fellow traders and tap into their wealth of experience by expanding your network—an invaluable resource for fresh perspectives and innovative methods. Continuously educating yourself through online courses, webinars, and reviewing reputable Forex materials will bolster your trading acumen. Embrace change and align yourself with current trends as a means to hone your craft; doing so not only adds depth to your understanding but also boosts your confidence to make informed trades. Remember, the journey of a Forex trader is not just about mastering strategies, but about evolving with the markets themselves.

The Importance of Continuing Education

In the ever-changing world of Forex trading, continuing education isn't just an advantage—it's a necessity. The financial markets are like a living organism, constantly evolving and adapting as new information becomes available. For those embarking on the journey of Forex trading, staying informed through ongoing education can be the difference between success and stagnation. It's about keeping your skills sharp, adapting to new market conditions, and always being ready to refine your strategies.

Forex trading is not a static field. Changes in the global economy, geopolitical events, and technological advancements influence market dynamics daily. As a trader, you must be proactive in seeking knowledge about these developments. By committing to continuous learning, you ensure that your understanding of concepts like currency pairs, leverage, and risk management isn't just resting on the information you started with but is expanding as the market shifts.

Among the many aspects of maintaining an educational mindset, embracing new resources is crucial. There are countless webinars, online courses, and workshops available that can keep you updated on the latest market trends. Joining trading forums and discussion groups can also provide insights from seasoned traders who've traversed the path you're on. Such community engagement is invaluable for exchanging ideas and gaining different perspectives on trading strategies.

Additionally, subscribing to financial news outlets and analysis reports can provide insights into macroeconomic trends that impact currency movements. By staying informed about global economic policies, interest rate changes, and other critical events, you can enhance your market analysis skills. This not only prepares you to speculate on future currency movements but also empowers you to make informed trading decisions.

It's also essential to recognize the role of self-reflection in continuous education. Keeping a trading journal can be one of the most powerful tools for learning. Documenting your trades, the reasons behind them, and their outcomes allows you to review and identify patterns over time. This practice helps in spotlighting your strengths and weaknesses, guiding your future trading decisions.

Furthermore, embracing technology is an integral part of evolving as a trader. Trading platforms and analytical tools are constantly updated with new features and capabilities. Familiarizing yourself with these tools ensures that you're leveraging the best available resources to enhance your trading. Whether it's new chart indicators or automated trading systems, understanding how to utilize these advancements can give you an edge.

However, continuing education is not just about the technical aspects of trading. Emotional discipline and mental resilience play a crucial role in your success. As you advance in your trading journey, engaging with literature or courses that focus on the psychology of trading can help you cultivate a more robust mindset. Being mentally prepared for the uncertainties of the market is as important as knowing the mechanics of executing trades.

In summing up, the path to becoming a successful Forex trader is paved with knowledge and adaptability. Continuing your education ensures you're not left behind as the market changes. It empowers you to make educated trading decisions backed by a comprehensive understanding of current global trends and market analysis techniques. By committing to lifelong learning, you place yourself in a position of continuous improvement and readiness, traits that are essential for thriving in the competitive world of Forex trading.

To conclude, always remember that your education as a trader doesn't stop once you grasp the fundamentals. The most successful traders are those who remain curious, open to learning, and ready to challenge their assumptions. By cultivating an ongoing education approach, you arm yourself with the tools needed to navigate the Forex market with confidence and foresight.

Networking with Other Traders

In the dynamic world of Forex trading, connecting with fellow traders can be one of the most significant catalysts for your success. Networking is not just about building contacts; it's about creating a community where knowledge and experiences are shared, successes are celebrated, and challenges are confronted together. As you dive into the network of Forex traders, you're not just joining a group—you're immersing yourself in a shared learning experience.

Foremost, networking provides a platform for learning and growth. Engaging with seasoned traders offers insights that books and courses might not cover. It's one thing to understand the theoretical concepts behind trading strategies, but it's another to hear firsthand from a trader who has faced real market conditions and emerged successfully. This firsthand knowledge—sometimes shared over a casual cup of coffee or in an energetic online forum—can reveal nuances and practical tips that might take years to discover on your own.

Beyond just gathering knowledge, networking enriches your experience by offering support during the highs and lows of trading. In the Forex market, where volatility is the norm, having a support system can help you stay grounded. Whether you experience the rush of a successful trade or the sting of an unexpected market turn, sharing these moments with a network of peers brings perspective and emotional resilience. Celebrating wins becomes more gratifying, and the burden of losses becomes lighter when you're not carrying them alone.

In today's digital age, the avenues for networking have expanded exponentially. From formal trading groups to social media platforms and online forums, access to diverse traders has never been easier. Twitter, for example, can be a goldmine for traders. Follow key influencers, participate in discussions, or just absorb the perspectives shared through posts and threads. Online platforms like these create virtual trading floors, bustling with ideas and debates.

Attend trading seminars and workshops when possible. These events are not only academically enriching but also provide face-to-face networking opportunities with industry veterans and fellow novices. The discussions and interactions here won't just enhance your understanding; they'll also build lasting professional relationships.

Moreover, networking isn't just about gaining from others; it's a two-way street. Sharing your insights and experiences can also solidify your understanding and refine your insights. Engaging actively in discussions, offering critiques, or sharing your trades and strategies can strengthen your understanding and help carve your niche in the trading community.

Local meetups and Forex trading clubs are also valuable. These groups often feature guest speakers, live trading sessions, and peer analysis, offering a rich blend of education and social interaction. Such environments encourage collective brainstorming and problem-solving, often sparking fresh ideas and approaches that you might never consider on your own.

Mentorship is another invaluable element of networking. Finding a mentor who can guide you, answer questions, and provide feedback can significantly accelerate your growth. A mentor can introduce you to the subtleties of trading styles, risk management, and market analysis, offering a more nuanced understanding than any textbook. They can provide the reassurance that comes from experience, offering a steadying hand when market conditions turn unpredictable.

Nevertheless, it's crucial to approach networking with purpose and authenticity. Building genuine relationships, rather than merely collecting contacts, creates a more supportive and meaningful network. Be genuinely interested in others' trading journeys, understand their strategies, and appreciate their challenges. Such authenticity fosters trust and mutual respect, which are the bedrock of enduring professional relationships.

Finally, remember that in networking, as in trading, consistency is key. Regular interaction ensures you remain informed about market trends and shifts in trading strategies. Being an active participant will ensure that your knowledge remains relevant and your strategies stay agile. The Forex market doesn't stand still, and neither should your connections within it.

Networking with other traders is more than just an exercise in social interaction. It's a strategic endeavor that, if approached with the right mindset and objectives, can significantly enhance your trading journey. As you continue to build your network, you'll find that the collective wisdom and support within these communities can empower you to navigate the Forex markets with greater confidence and competence.

Keeping Up with Market News and Trends

In the dynamic world of Forex trading, staying updated with market news and trends is crucial for making informed trades. This ever-evolving market responds to a myriad of factors, from economic indicators and geopolitical events to shifts in market sentiment. As a budding trader, embedding the habit of monitoring these trends not only sharpens your analytical skills but also enhances your ability to anticipate potential market movements. Subscribe to reputable financial news outlets, explore diverse resources, and engage with insights from seasoned traders. This proactive approach ensures you're not caught off guard when news impacts currency values. By integrating a perpetual learning mindset alongside your foundational knowledge, you position yourself to adapt strategically and thrive in the Forex landscape.

Online Review Request for This Book We'd love for you to share your thoughts and insights on how 'Keeping Up with Market News and Trends' has enhanced your journey into Forex trading by leaving a review online—your feedback inspires others and helps us continuously improve our content for all eager learners.

Conclusion

As we reach the conclusion of this journey into the dynamic world of Forex trading, it's essential to reflect on the knowledge and tools we've covered. From understanding the basic structure of currency pairs to grasping complex trading strategies, you're now equipped with the foundational insights needed to enter and evolve in the Forex market confidently. But remember, knowledge is only powerful when applied. The real challenge—and reward—lies in turning these insights into actionable strategies.

Forex trading is not just about making profits; it's about mastering the market's ebbs and flows. It's this rhythm, this constant dance between currency strength and weakness, that you've learned to analyze using both fundamental and technical strategies. The importance of consistently updating your skills cannot be overstated. Markets evolve, news unfolds, and trends shift. Being informed and adapting to these changes is crucial for long-term success.

Your journey in Forex trading won't be without its trials. The psychological aspects of trading—emotional discipline, overcoming fears, and cultivating a trader's mindset—are as important as any technical knowledge. As we've discussed, maintaining composure and making informed decisions during volatile market conditions can be the deciding factor between profit and loss.

Throughout this book, we've also addressed risk management, which is undeniably a cornerstone of successful trading. No strategy is complete without a clear understanding of how to protect your capital.

By implementing stop-loss and take-profit orders, you safeguard your funds while giving your trades the buffer they need to potentially succeed. Always trade within your means, making sure leverage is used wisely and not excessively, especially during the early stages of your trading career.

Another vital consideration is the creation and refinement of your personalized trading plan. This plan acts as your roadmap, guiding your trading decisions and helping you stay disciplined amidst market chaos. A strong trading plan incorporates all elements that impact your trading style and objectives, including risk tolerance, trading frequency, and preferred analysis methods.

Choosing the right Forex broker and platform is also fundamental to your success. The right broker offers not just fair spreads and good leverage options, but also reliable support and an intuitive platform. Your trading platform will be your launchpad into the market, and understanding how to use it effectively—whether through demo accounts or live trading—is essential for seamless trading execution.

The Forex market offers boundless opportunities, but it also requires diligence and perseverance. As emphasized in the preceding chapters, Forex trading is a continuous education. Staying informed through continuing education and networking with other traders can provide insights that drastically improve your trading approach. Don't shy away from learning from others' experiences or sharing your insights, as these interactions can be invaluable.

As you embark on your trading journey, keep a curious mind and an open willingness to adapt. Use the resources provided, revisit the foundational concepts when necessary, and always strive to adapt and grow. The insights gained here are merely a foundation—building expertise will require dedication and an unwavering commitment to learning. Remember, persistence and informed decision-making are your allies in the pursuit of consistent trading success.

In conclusion, Forex trading is an exciting venture filled with both possibilities and challenges. The skills and strategies you've learned will serve as your guideposts, while your passion and commitment will drive your journey forward. With this knowledge in hand, the Forex market is no longer a distant realm but a space you've begun to understand and navigate. Your path may differ from others, and that's perfectly okay. Embrace your unique journey, continue to learn, and let the Forex market unfold its opportunities before you.

Appendix A: Appendix

In this appendix, we've compiled essential resources and supplementary materials to aid your journey into the Forex trading world. Think of this section as your trusted companion, providing tools and references that reinforce the concepts discussed throughout the book. Here, you'll find recommendations for books, online courses, and forums where seasoned traders congregate, all tailored to enrich your understanding and skills in Forex trading. These resources are curated to ensure that they're both accessible to newcomers and aligned with current market trends. As you continue to progress, this appendix will serve as your go-to guide, encouraging you to apply what you've learned with confidence and wisdom. Whether it's seeking deeper insights into technical analysis or connecting with a community of like-minded individuals, let this appendix be your springboard to advanced proficiency and sustained growth in the Forex market.

Glossary of Forex Terms

Welcome to the Glossary of Forex Terms! Whether you're diving into the world of forex trading or brushing up on your understanding, this glossary aims to clarify key terms that are essential in forex trading. Grasping these concepts will not only boost your confidence but also empower you to make more informed trading decisions.

Ask Price

The ask price is the price a seller is willing to accept for a currency pair. It's essentially the inverse of the bid price and represents the cost you need to pay to purchase the base currency. The ask price is always higher than the bid price in normal market conditions.

Base Currency

In any forex pair, the base currency is the first currency listed. For example, in the pair EUR/USD, the euro is the base currency. Your trading decisions often revolve around the strength or weakness of this currency relative to the quote currency.

Bid Price

The bid price is the price a buyer is willing to pay for a currency pair. It's the price at which you can sell the base currency in exchange for the quote currency. The bid is always lower than the ask price to allow for profit margins for market makers.

Broker

A forex broker is an intermediary that provides you access to a trading platform for buying and selling currency pairs. Brokers may offer different services and fee structures, so it's crucial to choose one that aligns with your trading goals.

Currency Pair

A currency pair is the quotation of two different currencies, with the value of one currency being quoted against the other. Common pairs include EUR/USD, GBP/USD, and USD/JPY. Understanding how to read and interpret a currency pair is fundamental to forex trading.

Leverage

Leverage is a powerful tool in forex trading that allows you to control a large position with a relatively small amount of capital. While leverage can magnify profits, it equally increases the risk of significant losses, so using it wisely is essential.

Lot

A lot represents the standardized size of a transaction in forex trading. Typically, a standard lot equals 100,000 units of the base currency. Familiarity with different lot sizes, such as mini and micro lots, can help you manage your risk effectively.

Margin

Margin is the collateral a trader must deposit to open a trading position, serving as a good-faith deposit. Adequate margin ensures your broker that you can cover potential losses on a trade. Always keep an eye on your margin requirements to avoid unexpected liquidations.

Pip

A pip, short for "percentage in point," is the smallest price move in a currency pair's exchange rate. For most pairs, a pip is the fourth decimal place. Knowing how to calculate pip values can aid in analyzing profit and loss potential in trades.

Quote Currency

The quote currency is the second currency listed in a currency pair and represents the amount needed to buy one unit of the base currency. It plays a critical role in determining the pair's price direction and trading decisions.

Spread

The spread is the difference between the bid and ask price of a currency pair. It's a key factor in determining your trading costs, as a smaller spread can lead to more profitable trades over time.

Arming yourself with these terms will pave the way to a deeper understanding of how the forex market operates. As you continue to explore forex trading, keep revisiting these definitions to reinforce your knowledge and support your trading journey.

Recommended Resources for Further Learning

Embarking on your journey into the world of Forex can feel quite overwhelming, with its sea of unfamiliar terms and concepts. While this book aims to provide you with a solid foundation, there's a wealth of resources available to help deepen your understanding and refine your skills. Let's dive into some highly recommended resources that will pave the way for further exploration and mastery of Forex trading.

First and foremost, online courses and webinars offer structured, flexible learning environments. Websites like *Coursera* and *Udemy* host courses tailored to various skill levels. Whether you're diving into the basics or exploring advanced strategies, these platforms provide interactive content including quizzes and assignments that reinforce learning. Additionally, consider attending live webinars hosted by experts. They not only cover current market trends but also offer real-time Q&A sessions, allowing you to clarify doubts on the fly.

Books remain a timeless resource for learning and reflection. For comprehensive guides, consider titles like "Forex For Beginners" by Anna Coulling and "Currency Trading For Dummies" by Brian Dolan. These books break down complex concepts into digestible pieces and provide invaluable insights into both the technical and psychological aspects of trading. If you're already familiar with the basics, books focusing on specific areas of interest, such as technical analysis or trading psychology, can be quite enriching.

Podcasts have become an increasingly popular medium for learning. They allow you to absorb valuable information on the go. By tuning into shows such as "Forex Q&A" or "The Trading Coach Podcast," you can stay updated with market analysis, hear success stories, and gain motivation from seasoned traders. Podcasts often feature interviews with industry experts, offering diverse perspectives and fostering a holistic understanding of Forex markets.

Don't underestimate the power of communities and forums in the learning process. Platforms like *BabyPips* and *Forex Factory* serve as meeting grounds for traders worldwide, from novices to veterans. Engaging with these communities allows you to ask questions, share experiences, and gain insights into trading strategies that have worked for others. Active participation in such forums not only enhances your learning curve but also builds your network, enabling knowledge exchange on a global scale.

Another potential avenue for advancement is mentorship. Connecting with a seasoned trader can provide personalized guidance. A mentor can offer tailored advice, help you navigate challenges, and keep you accountable. While finding a suitable mentor requires effort, local trading groups or online forums are good places to start your search. Remember, mentorship doesn't have to occur within a formal hierarchy; often, mutual learning occurs as knowledge and experiences are shared.

To stay abreast of current events and market sentiments, subscribe to financial news platforms such as *Bloomberg* and *Reuters*. These sites frequently publish articles examining economic indicators, geopolitical events, and general market trends impacting Forex. Additionally, leverage the analytical reports provided by reputable Forex brokers; these often come with insights that can refine your trading decisions.

Finally, demo accounts offered by many trading platforms are indispensable for practice. They simulate real market conditions without financial risk, allowing you to test strategies, familiarize yourself with trading software, and hone your technical skills. Regular practice in a demo environment can bridge the gap between theoretical knowledge and real-world application.

In summary, whether you're interacting with a community, reading a well-respected book, or practicing on a demo account, each resource plays a crucial role in enriching your Forex education. Continuous learning is the key to becoming a successful trader. Set small, regular goals for further education, and stay curious and informed. Armed with these resources and an eager mindset, you're well-prepared to grow and adapt in the ever-evolving landscape of Forex trading.

www.ingramcontent.com/pod-product-compliance
Lightning Source LLC
LaVergne TN
LVHW100332210926
848480LV00003B/1312